Leadership Simple

Leading People To Lead Themselves

THE PRACTICE OF LEAD MANAGEMENT

Steve Morris / Jill Morris

IMPOREX INTERNATIONAL INC.
SAN DIEGO, CALIFORNIA

Published By Imporex International, Inc.
200 Harbor Drive, 1601
San Diego, California CA 92101-6848

Book Design by Idea Engineering, Inc.

PUBLISHER'S CATALOGING-IN-PUBLICATION

Morris, Steve
Leadership simple : leading people to lead themselves : the practice of lead management / Steve Morris, Jill Morris. -- 1st ed.
p. cm.
Includes index
LCCN 2003103972
Casebound ISBN: 978-0-9740320-1-6
Paperback ISBN: 978-0-9740320-2-3
eBook ISBN: 978-0-9740320-3-0

1. Leadership. 2. Management. I. Morris, Jill, II. Title.

HD57.7.M68 2003 658.4'092

Printed in the United States of America
10 9 8 7 6 5 4 3 2

Special Sales: *Leadership Simple* is available for bulk purchases at a discount for corporate and organizational use.
Contact us at *books@choiceworks.com*

DEDICATION

Leadership Simple *is dedicated to all the visionary leaders who have applied these ideas in their lives to make a difference in the worlds of work, family, and friends.*

Ann,
Thank you for caring about how you lead and for making a difference. May you continue to grow as you continue your journey.
Love,
Jue

CONTENTS

INTRODUCTION

Lead Management

Leaders are people who other people follow.

Some leaders are command-and-control demagogues, and a few lead with the gentle touch of a brain surgeon. Some great leaders don't know they are leading at all. No matter what their styles, in each extreme and in between there are leaders who create the intended results and those who do not. Style has little to do with it.

Some leaders use their power and their ability to strike fear in their followers. They do this at a cost of both psychological and physical pain to most everyone around them, including themselves.

Great leaders inspire others to follow through their words and actions. They lead people to lead themselves. The people they lead want to follow and want to do the best job they can for their own satisfaction, not because they fear reprisal. They learn from their leaders. Those who follow great leaders, in the long run, always outperform those who are led with a heavy hand.

In looking at the leaders we've worked with in over forty years of business, we've found one characteristic that stands out in all the great ones: the ability to self-evaluate and lead others to do the same. We call this Lead Management. Lead Management is about leading by applying a simple process of self-evaluation.

The process we demonstrate and explain in this book is easy to learn. It is simple because most of what we suggest, you already know how to do. If you can visualize a simple map, ask questions, listen to answers, and then generate new questions and alternatives, you can put this process to work and become an extraordinary leader who creates results without coercion.

There are obstacles to putting this process to use in your life. You will have to leave behind the comfort of some old habits to allow new ones to arise; observe and evaluate your choices of behavior and perceptions; become deliberate about what you want when you choose a course of action. We show you how to do that in our story.

Lead Management is a practice. You learn by using the process over and over again. Anyone who has the resolve and is willing to continually practice using the tools we provide will create new habits of effective leadership, produce results, and inspire followers to ever-increasing performance. If you practice Lead Management, you will win great rewards and get what you want.

The story we tell in this book is presented in the form of a conversation. The conversation is a composite of many exchanges we've had with leaders in all kinds of organizations.

It is remotely possible to have a single conversation like the one that takes place in the morning of this story and create the kind of transformation that occurs for Jerry, our main character. But he is only at the beginning of a long journey and a way of being we call Lead Management. We welcome you to that beginning.

ACKNOWLEDGMENT

Dr. William Glasser

The information we present in this book is based on Choice Theory. Choice Theory has evolved over forty-five years from the observations and work of Dr. William Glasser.

Dr. Glasser is a psychiatrist by training and practice. He is a leader in believing that people have the ability to choose what they want and the behaviors they use to get it. In other words, Dr. Glasser teaches that we are not captives of our histories, our emotions, or our habits. We always have a choice.

Dr. Glasser coined the term "Lead Management" to describe the application of his work to the environment of organizations.

The authors are both graduates of the William Glasser Institute, where we've been certified in Choice Theory.

As businesspeople we have learned to interpret, adapt, and use Dr. Glasser's theories for everyday application to organizational challenges. Our clients have learned to be accountable and take ownership for the results they create alone and in cooperation with others.

We are grateful to Dr. Glasser and all the fine trainers in his institute who helped us refine our own work to form a new approach to Lead Management and Choice Theory in the business world.

1

The Rat Race

It's not true that life is one damn thing after another; it is one damn thing over and over.

—Edna St. Vincent Millay

"What do you want, Jerry?"

"I don't want people looking over my shoulder. Did Sam send you to New York to fix me? If so, it's not going to work. I don't need fixing."

Jerry gets up from his chair behind the desk piled with stacks of papers, some of them hanging precariously over the edge. Two stained coffee cups and an open bottle of aspirin sit at one corner. He begins to pace the room while he tucks in the tail of his shirt, pulls up his pants onto his ample belly, and runs his hand over the top of his nearly smooth head.

He continues to talk. Fast. "I have too many things to get done and not enough time to do them. My sales force brings in orders. Production and engineering don't respond unless they have something negative to say. I spend my time on the phone with customers, engineers, and administrators putting out fires. I have a new product launch that is due at the end of the month. Every day there are half a dozen meetings, all of which I'm expected to attend, some of them scheduled for the same times. What are they thinking? I'm the only one who can take care of all this? Max, I don't have time for you today and maybe never."

"Sounds like you are overwhelmed. I can understand your frustration. Too much to do, too little time to do it in, and not enough resources to boot. Isn't that true?"

"Of course, it's true. It's the same for all of us. Damn digital time and we're not even in the internet business. It's a rat race. Everyone wants everything yesterday," he says as he falls back in his chair, exhausted by his own agitation.

2

The Territory of Choice

I think there is a choice possible to us at any moment, as long as we live.

—Muriel Rukeyser

My name is Max. I work out of Santa Barbara for the corporation. They send me to places to solve problems, assist people, get them back on track. Like most managers today, I'm a combination of coach, trainer, leader, manager, worker, and jack-of-all-trades.

Jerry is partially right. The boss, Sam Palmer, CEO, chairman, and founder of the corporation, does expect me to "fix" the situation, but he is not of the mind that people need fixing.

I can visualize and hear Sam, in that deep gravelly voice of his, as he leans back, pulls the pipe from his mouth, looks toward the sky through the big floor-to-ceiling window in his office as he says, "People are doing the best they can at any given moment. They just get lost in their own thoughts and fears. They need a little help to figure things out. To connect what they want with what the organization wants. Max, go to New York and help this guy. Get him to start looking at himself instead of all those situations and predicaments."

So that's what I do. I go to New York or Fargo or Geneva and get people to self-evaluate, because that's the edge that gets them what they want. What do I mean by self-evaluation? I train and coach people to make productive choices by teaching them to explore their behaviors, perceptions, and wants. I help them connect the results they create to the actions they take.

If they're not looking at themselves, if they blame things, people, and events outside themselves for the results they create, then they cannot be expected to influence people and events in ways that make a difference for themselves and the corporation.

Jerry Green is the national sales manager in one of our business units located in New York. He excels at his job. Business is exploding, but good support people are hard to find, and he has what I call a classic problem with other departments in the organization. But I'll get to all of that.

Anytime I go out on an assignment, I like to self-evaluate, to look at what I know about myself in relation to the situation and the corporation. I use a model of human behavior I call the Triangle of Choice that actually represents the operating system of human thought and action — something like Microsoft Windows® or a MAC OS.

The Triangle of Choice is a map of how people organize the information they receive, what they do with it, and the actions they take as a result.

It begins with the concept that we form perceptions based on information we receive through our five senses. We combine that information with the experiences of our past to form a picture of our current reality. Everything we see, hear, taste, touch, and smell combines with what we already know to form this picture of our personal reality. We call the picture our perceptions.

Triangle of Choice

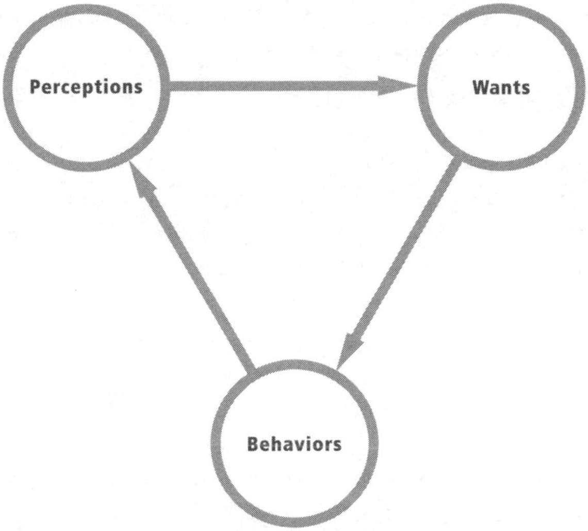

Biologists Humberto R. Maturana and Francisco J. Varella have observed that at least 80 percent of what we perceive to be information from our outside world actually comes from what we already know, from the experiences we hold inside our memories. We sense some event or thing and then we draw from our knowledge additional data to fill in what we missed in the original communication or information. Or, we select out what is not consistent with what we know and replace it with knowledge we already have.

When I talked to Jerry on the phone to set up the appointment, he was rushing to a meeting. His words were slurred together like they were coming out of a machine gun. "Nine A.M. on Monday morning is OK, but I need to keep it short because I'm busy." Click! He was gone.

Sam Palmer shared his impressions and concern for Jerry, saying, "He's a star performer who can deliver big volume. Seems to be agitated and out of sorts these days. Sounds like he is about to implode."

My impulse is to interpret what others say without checking it out with them. It is easy to believe my first impression rather than verify or review what I know. But this does not produce the results I want.

From the conversation with Jerry I may have jumped to the conclusion that he was rude, self-absorbed, and out of control. Adding what Sam said gave me a picture of a man who was under pressure. "Under pressure" is a label I put on the various pieces of information I received from Jerry and Sam.

There is one thing I've learned in my practice of self-evaluation: my perceptions, like those of others, are not always accurate. Whenever I label a person or a situation with words like "under pressure," "emergency," and "problem," I oversimplify, categorize, and generalize in a manner that may not serve me or the people I want to assist. The label puts people and events in a nice tidy box, whether it will help or not. Then I can deal with the people or situation using some formulaic approach that will relieve the pressure, end the emergency, or solve the problem if I just do one, two, and three or A, B, and C.

Nothing is further from the truth.

The facts I have about Jerry are that he talks fast,

says he is in a hurry, always produces above his quota, and Sam Palmer judges that he will implode — an evaluation of Jerry without supporting evidence.

If I can keep my perceptions about Jerry and his situation as close as possible to the raw data I received and be aware of the judgments and conclusions I am drawing, then I may be able to observe how he perceives the situation and help him and the corporation get what they want.

This is the point about perceptions. We choose the meaning of the information we receive. I could say Jerry was under pressure. What would his interpretation be?

Checking out the accuracy of my perceptions is the first step in my self-evaluation. "Perceptions" are the first corner of the Triangle of Choice.

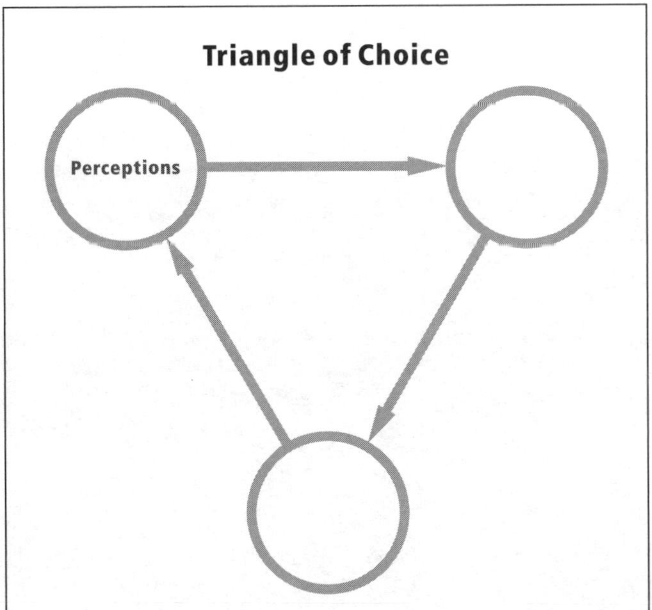

I want Jerry to be and feel successful in his job, to stay open to his interpretation of the situation. I want to lead him to self-evaluate proactively. I want to teach Jerry how to use the Triangle of Choice.

The second corner of the Triangle of Choice is what we "Want."

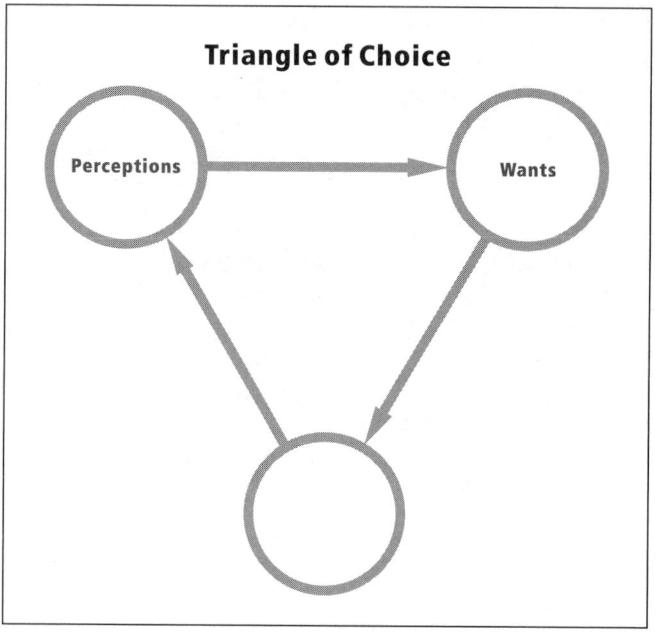

Triangle of Choice

Whenever there is a difference between my perceptions of the situation and what I want in the moment, there is a "gap." I want Jerry to be successful, and I do not perceive that he feels successful right now. That is my gap in this moment.

I will not know if Jerry shares the same gap until I ask him.

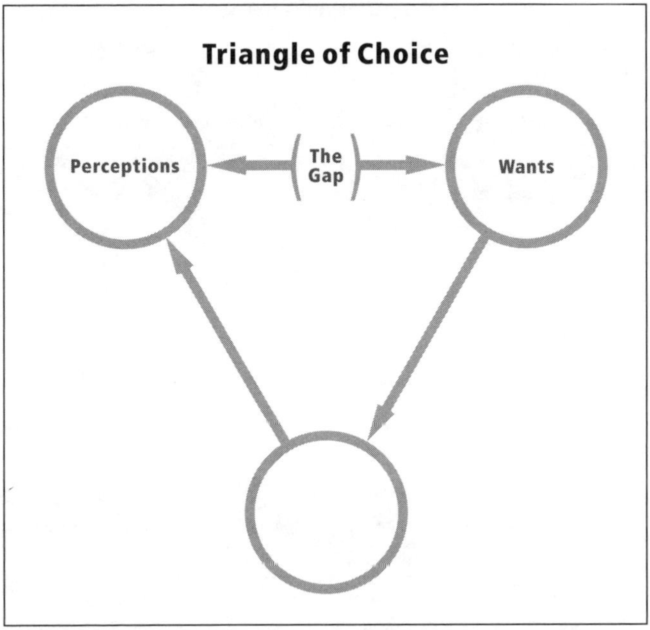

When I have a gap, I take action to close the gap, and that action is always in the form of behavior. I choose a behavior to close the gap between what I want and what I perceive I have. The behaviors I choose do not always create the results I want. "Behavior" is the third corner of the Triangle of Choice.

Triangle of Choice

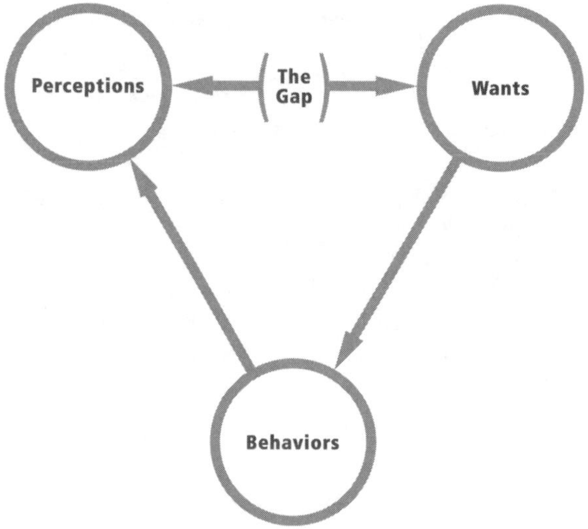

The behavior I will choose with Jerry is to ask questions that uncover what he wants, what he perceives, and the behaviors he is choosing to get what he wants. This will help him self-evaluate.

I will teach him to use these tools in a positive atmosphere of support. I will demonstrate how the tools work in the actions I take and in working with him on his real-time issues. My goal is to help Jerry get what he wants and meet the company's needs.

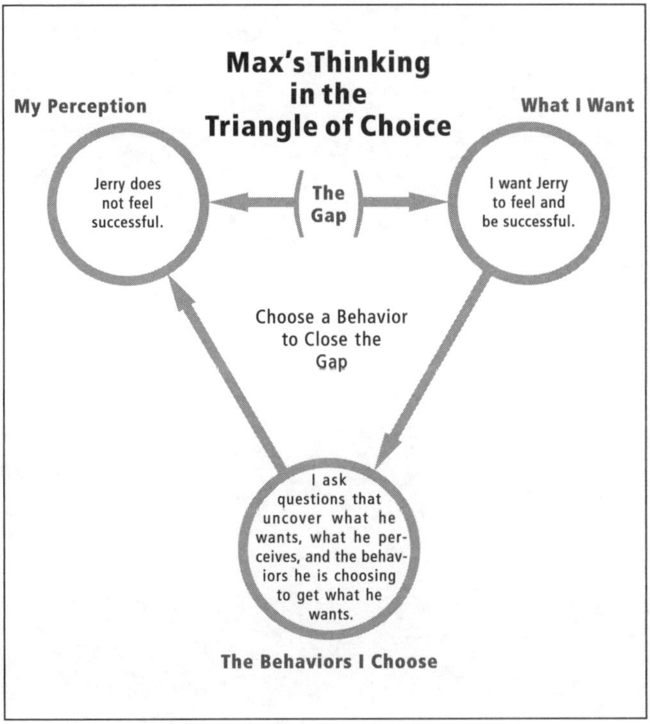

3

What Do You Want?

The first step to getting the things you want out of life is this: decide what you want.

—Ben Stein

After his outpouring of frustration, I ask my opening question again in a slightly different form. "Jerry, how would you like things to be?" (Meaning, what do you want?)

"What I don't want is all this infighting, the meetings, the power plays between departments. We're in it together." Jerry is stabbing the air with his finger as he speaks. "If I have to go to one more of Arthur Himple's staff meetings, I'll bust. Don't get me wrong. He's a great person, but his meetings produce little action. I've just given up."

He takes a deep breath and releases it. "I sit there, listen, and contribute nothing unless I'm asked." Jerry reaches for a coffee cup, takes a swig, and then wipes his mouth with the back of his hand.

"Jerry, so far you have told me what you do not want. Would you go to the supermarket with a list of what you do not want, expecting to come home with what you want?"

He smiles at me. "I guess it doesn't make any sense, but there are things I don't want to be doing."

"What you do not want is helpful up to a point. It gives me a picture of how you perceive the situation. What you have described — is it an accurate picture of what is happening around you?"

Jerry sighs. "Yes. I am overwhelmed by the problems, the ineffectiveness of people, and the lack of cooperation. I've never felt this way before and I don't like it." His arms stretch over his head as if he is reaching to the heavens for some divine guidance.

"Would it help you right now to figure out what you do want, Jerry? Your vision of how you want things to be?"

"I guess it would help to get specific." He takes a moment to think, grabbing a yellow pad and a gold pen, scribbling something. The notes don't seem to have anything to do with our current conversation because he drops the pad when he finishes and looks up at me.

"What I want first is more time to work with my sales managers and salespeople. Help them improve their selling skills, get more sales. That is my job and I have always done it well. I see great opportunities out in the field and we're not leveraging them to build our business. I cannot build the business if I am putting out fires and all this other crap."

"Jerry, I'm going to summarize what you have said. You believe your job is to get more business and make the company grow. You want the time and the right

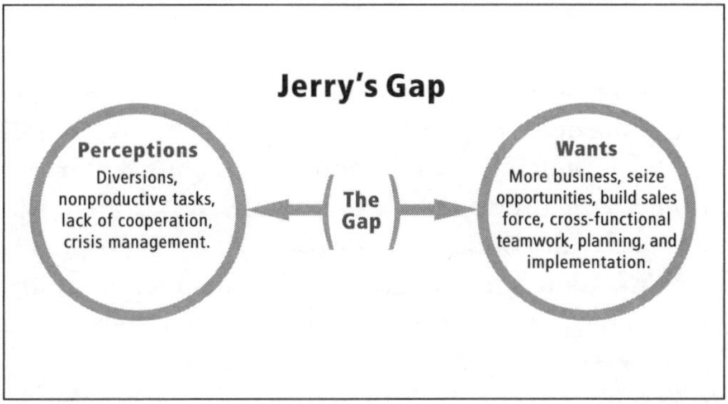

to focus so you can do your job. You want to seize opportunities, build your sales force, and create cross-functional teamwork. You would like to replace crisis management with a stable approach to planning and implementation.

"What you perceive you have are too many diversions and nonproductive things to do that interfere with your capacity to create the outcomes you want. Is that true?"

"Max, you said it better than I did. Isn't that what Sam Palmer wants, too? To build the business?"

"He does and he wants you to succeed with your goals. You have a gap between what you want — to build the business — and what you perceive you have — too many nonproductive, crisis-driven events and requests.

"Whenever there is a gap between what you most want and what you perceive you have, you are motivated to close that gap. All behaviors are your best attempt in the moment to close a gap between what you think you have and what you want. What are you doing to close that gap, Jerry?"

"What do you mean?" Jerry surveys his desk for a moment. He reaches across the sea of papers and picks up a large pile, holding them in his outstretched hand toward me.

"All day long I respond to requests, to the needs of others, the details of the business. Look at my calendar." He drops the pile he is holding and pushes a large printed page toward me. I see boxes for every hour of the day filled with notes to call people or go to meetings.

"Max, there's not a single thing scheduled with my sales managers, my salespeople, or with a customer. These are all internal meetings and reports I have to deal with."

"What you are saying to me, Jerry, is that you do not have time to schedule any actions that will create business or develop your people, because you are spending all your time on other situations."

"If I don't deal with these situations, our products will not get delivered. My salespeople want their orders processed and delivered, and everyone else wants me to provide information. They all want me to help them solve problems and plan for the future."

"Are you doing anything else to get what you want?"

"No." Jerry shakes his head from side to side, his face contorted as if in pain. Leaning toward me, punctuating each word with his stabbing finger, he says slowly, "I don't have the time."

"So, Jerry, is any of this getting you what you want? Is it working?"

He thinks for a moment. "In some ways, I guess. I get the deliveries out and solve some of the problems. That is something I want. But that's all. Not very creative, is it?"

"Creativity is important to you?"

"Creating sales. That is what I'm about."

"Is there anything you are currently doing to create

the sales you want?"

"I talk to my people in regard to solving problems, but nothing real creative. It's more like putting out fires and keeping what we already have. There's little planning except the budget process and a few rough ideas we throw together at the beginning of each year. Little time for reflection."

"Jerry, what else could you do to get what you want?"

"I don't have time to do anything else."

"You need more time to generate sales and work with your people?"

"I can't put in any more time than I am now: ten to twelve hours a day, six days a week. That's enough."

"What else could you do with the time you put in?"

"It's the only way, Max. I have to use my time differently."

"Do you want to change the way you allocate your time?"

"I do, but I can't see how."

"Pull out that calendar you showed me earlier. If you had what you wanted, what would be scheduled tomorrow instead of what is on there now?"

Jerry shakes his head again and picks up the calendar. "There is Arthur's staff meeting at 9:00 A.M. Then there are two meetings with production and order processing to go over their latest schedules and problems. That pretty much takes care of the morning. Then . . ."

I hold up my hand and climb out of the deep leather chair I've been sitting in. "Jerry. Stop right there. Let's look at the morning. If you had your perfect schedule, what would you be doing to drive for more sales?"

I lean on his desk as he speaks. "I would be on the phone with my four regional managers talking about their plans for the next quarter. Listening to the steps they are taking to build business. Giving them guidance. Helping them see the things I see that can improve our numbers. Coaching them on their performance." I can hear Jerry's enthusiasm as he speaks, see the change in his face, his posture. This is what Jerry loves.

"How would this improve your numbers?"

"I would be leading them to lead their people. I would call some of our top performers. Give them a boost; share my vision with them. I like to stay in touch with these people because they respond to my direct contact and it gives me a firsthand picture of what is happening in the field."

He rises out of his chair, facing me. "You know, Max, I'd call a couple of key customers who I used to talk to all the time." He stabs the air again. "Keep a finger on the pulse and make sure that we are doing the right things for them."

"Jerry, these sound like the right things to be doing, to use your term. What stands in your way of doing them tomorrow?"

"I have these meetings."

"What is the purpose of these meetings?"

"To work out solutions to problems and plan for the future. The sales department needs to be represented so that we get deliveries out and have input into future decisions."

"Do you personally have to represent the sales department?"

"I only have a small staff here: my administrative assistant and a couple of lower-level people. My inside salespeople."

"Are these other people incapable of representing

sales at these meetings?"

"They'll lose time. Get behind in their work."

"Whose time is more valuable to the company?"

Still standing, Jerry scans the office and then his desk. The room is quiet except for the air whispering through the vent in the ceiling. It seems like five minutes before he responds. "Never thought of it that way. Maybe there are some alternatives."

"Can you think of a few, Jerry?"

"I could ask them to send me a copy of the minutes and then email my responses and suggestions."

"Would that be effective for you and Arthur?"

"Probably not. Sales and operations need some interaction to get things accomplished. I could sit in on a phone conference while I work on paperwork from my office."

"Would that really give you the time you are looking for?"

"No, it would just be distracting and not respectful of the other people in the meeting. I guess I can send Angela, my admin, to the meetings with production and order processing. She's a good negotiator. She is great with the details. She likes meetings. She usually ends up doing the grunt work after the meetings anyway."

He drops back down into his chair. "We can skip the staff meeting tomorrow. It's Arthur's meeting. He may be pissed but I could go to the next one."

"What is the purpose of the meeting?"

"Arthur runs this division. We discuss the operational problems of the week. He is not very organized. He leads long discussions that never result in solutions. There are rarely any agreements. When people do agree to do something, no one holds them accountable for the results. We end up discussing the same things over and over."

"You didn't answer my question, Jerry. Do you know the purpose of the meeting?"

"Oh, I guess to solve problems."

"Solving these problems; is that something you want?"

"Getting them solved is important, and I have no control over what happens in operations."

"Is it more important to focus on your sales efforts or solving operational problems?"

"Sales. No doubt there."

"Then, how can you show Arthur that you value his intent and still not go?"

"I can tell him in advance that I have other pressing issues to deal with tomorrow. I can ask my internal sales supervisor, Billy Farnsworth, to attend the meeting and see what Arthur's reaction is."

"Is that a good permanent solution?"

"It's good for this week. I'll look at how I can rearrange other days, like we're doing now. See how Billy does."

"Great! You have identified some alternatives to carve out this one morning. These are just possibilities. What are you actually going to do?"

"Maxine! You are one tough woman. You just pin a guy down to every detail, don't you?"

"That is why they pay me the big bucks, Jerry."

He lifts the phone and asks Angela to come into the office.

Angela arrives, a petite woman, short dark spiky hair with blond tips, tight jeans, a bright red silk blouse and red shoes to match.

"Yeah, boss, whaddaya got?" She turns to me. "Oh,

hi, Max. You're early. I didn't know it was you in here." She does a quick scan from feet to hair, a big smile on her face. "Cool outfit, Maxine. I like that snazzy suit." Gum cracks in her mouth. Then she turns to Jerry.

"Angela, please call Billy and ask him to sit in for me at the staff meeting tomorrow. Then call Arthur's admin and tell her about the substitution."

Jerry looks at me for some kind of reaction. I nod.

"I would like you to take on more responsibility around production and order processing. You substitute for me at those two meetings tomorrow. It works out; you can handle those functions for me in the future. That is, if you want to."

"Jerry, I'm glad to do it. It'll take you out of the middle and give me a chance to deal directly with all these guys I talk to on the phone ten times a day. It'll build my influence with them."

"Thank you. One other thing."

"What's that, boss?"

"Starting at 9:00 A.M. tomorrow, set up forty-five-minute telephone appointments with each of the four regional managers. I want to fill up the free time we've just made. Give me about fifteen minutes between each. Start on the East Coast and work your way across the country. I'll work through lunch."

"No problem, boss. Anything else?" Angela finishes taking notes. "I'll put them on the calendar as they confirm and get back to you on any problems. Do you want me to order lunch for you for tomorrow?"

"No, I'll play it by ear."

"Just make sure you eat," Angela said over her shoulder as she left the office.

I looked away from the door toward Jerry. He was erasing entries in his calendar in the computer. "What are you planning for the rest of this morning?" I ask.

"We have a meeting in a few minutes with two people from our IT division who want to show us a new system they will be installing for tracking inside sales activity. They wanted an hour."

"Jerry, we have developed some momentum. Do you want to continue our process or attend that meeting?"

"I promised them I'd attend, but it's really Billy's system. I can leave the discussion and decisions to him. I'll just take a few minutes with them in the beginning to get the meeting started. You can have a short break and then we'll continue."

4

Five Easy Questions

You can tell whether a man is clever by his answers.
You can tell whether a man is wise by his questions.

—Mahfouz Naguib

Ten minutes later we are back in Jerry's office.

I ask, "Is Tuesday morning a good time to set up these calls with your people every week?"

"I'll check it out with them."

"What could you do to reserve the time for these calls?"

"I can just do it. Cancel or reassign all my other obligations for Tuesdays or whatever day I choose. I'll do that tomorrow.

"Max, I want to thank you for this. I used to schedule my needs first on the calendar, but things just crept up on me. I lost control to everyone else. Without your help I would never have seen a way to get some time for my work, the work I want to be doing."

"Is this enough time to schedule for the work you

want to do, just one morning?"

"No. But it's a beginning."

"Do you want more time to focus on sales?"

"Yes, but I don't see how."

"Let's spend the morning figuring that out. I want to give you some information that will help you do this kind of self-evaluation we just went through together, to generate alternatives for some of your current choices. Then you can carve out the time you want and regain control over your productivity. Would you like that?"

"Definitely."

"Jerry, I want to explain the process we just went through. It is a formal, deliberate way of thinking that will lead you and the people you work with to self-evaluate and get the same kind of results we've just created. Do you want to learn about it?"

"Yes," Jerry says. "Let's get started now."

"Remember the first thing I asked you this morning?"

"Yes, I do. 'What do you want, Jerry?'"

"Right. It is the first in a series of questions I use over and over again in almost every session I have with the people I work with. It is the door into a person's thoughts.

"I have asked questions to assist you to see your perceptions, your wants, and your behaviors. I never told you to do anything. I just asked questions, made suggestions, and paraphrased some of what you said.

"You generated the alternative choices and you took action, applying behaviors to close the gap between what you wanted and what you perceived you had. You also changed your perceptions. You realized that you had other alternatives. Follow me so far?"

"What you're saying, Max, is that you were working from some kind of plan or map?"

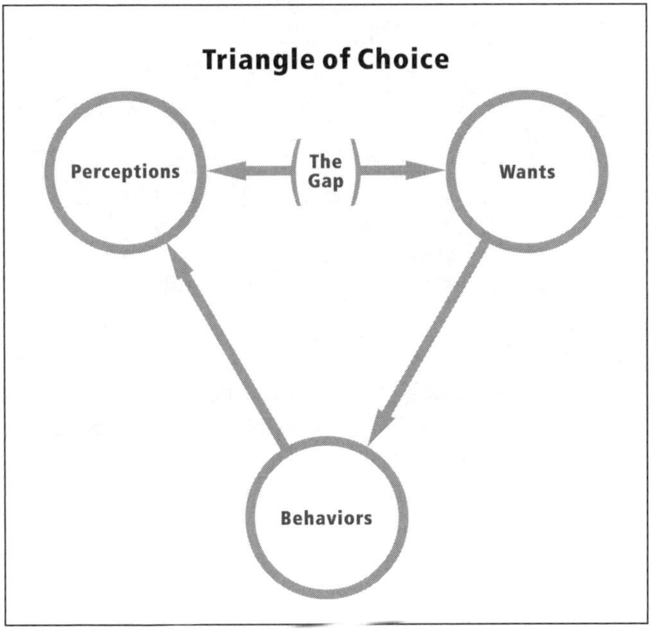

"Yes, Jerry, a very simple mental model. When any of us are stuck in a gap, we have three areas of leverage.

1. *We can change our perception.*
2. *We can change what we want.*
3. *We can change our behavior.*

"We can do one, two, or all three of these together to get what we want. These are the three elements of the Triangle of Choice. It is the mental model I work from.

"This morning so far I've asked only five questions in several different forms. They were all tied to recognizing and understanding your model of reality. They were:

1. *What do you want? (Wants)*
2. *What are you doing to get what you want? (Behavior)*
3. *Is it working to get you what you want? (Perception)*
4. *What else can you do? (Alternative behaviors)*
5. *What will you do? (Planned behaviors)*

"Come up here for a moment," I say to Jerry as I move toward his white board on the wall.

I begin to draw the diagram of the Triangle of Choice on the white board.

"These five questions we call the Procedures That Lead to Change. They are the keys to all self-evaluation. Even though I asked the questions, you did the evaluating. I guided you through this self-evaluation process, but the answers you gave were all yours. You could also ask the questions of yourself. You could be asking:

1. *What do I want?*
2. *What am I doing to get it?*
3. *Is it working?*
4. *What else can I do?*
5. *What will I do?*

"You can ask these questions in many forms, for example, to evaluate a past situation:

1. *What result were you after?*
2. *What actions did you take?*
3. *Did you create the kind of situation you wanted?*
4. *Can you see any alternatives to this course of action?*
5. *What do you plan to do next time?*

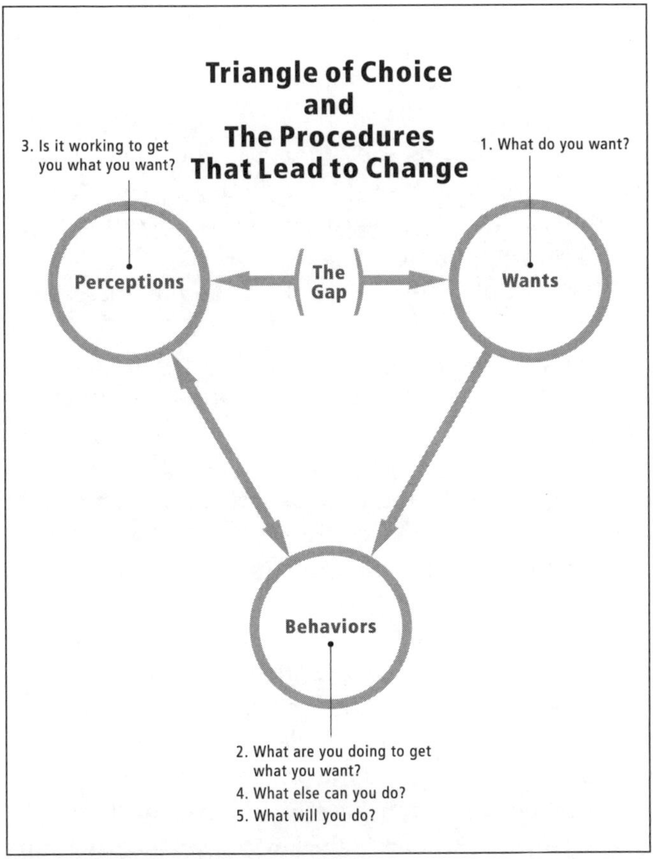

"When I ask these questions, I keep the image of the Triangle of Choice in my mind, tying the answers to the various components of the map.

"I do this deliberately. When I first started using the Triangle of Choice to lead people, I had to keep coming back to the mental model, over and over, to remind myself that this was the most effective tool I could use to assist myself and others in the process of self-evaluation. After months and years of practice, I no longer have to think of using this tool. It is where I go first to help myself and the people I work with.

"But when we start with new tools like the Triangle of Choice and the Procedures That Lead to Change, we need to make a conscious effort to apply them. That is what I am going to assist you to do this morning and in the future. I'm going to give you a box full of tools and then help you put them to work.

"How would it help you, Jerry, to put these tools to work?"

"Max, I've always spent time self-evaluating, as you call it. But I've never had any kind of formal system to guide me. So learning to use the Triangle of Choice and then applying it to my own plans and problems would add a structure to the process. Probably create more consistent results. I like it already."

"Are there other ways you could apply this knowledge, Jerry?"

He starts to pace the floor. "I could also teach the system to my own people so that they could learn to make choices that work more effectively for themselves and the organization. I could lead them with this kind of model. Am I leaving something out?"

"Actually, Jerry, you have hit the nail on the head. The Triangle of Choice is the key component in a simple system of leadership we call Lead Management.

"Lead Managers recognize that the best way to lead people is to help others self-evaluate. In reality, leadership is a conversation, a verbal journey between people. Lead Management is a system that permits leaders and the people they lead to navigate through the maze of each other's wants, perceptions, and behaviors. It is a template for a specific kind of conversation that drives business success through people, rather than in spite of them.

"When you ask questions, you lead people to think for themselves. They see how they can get what they want and how they can connect those wants with what the organization needs. You lead them to connect their map of reality with the maps of other people and the organization.

"Lead Management replaces boss management. Boss managers tell people what to do, rather than lead them through a process of self-evaluation. Boss managers cut off the learning process that creates consistent high-performance results. They coerce rather than lead. Lead Management inspires."

"Sounds like a lot of leverage from just a few questions and a picture of a triangle. And, I think it's pretty basic, Max. I know this stuff."

"Jerry, I am not talking about knowing. How often do you use these specific questions?"

"Well, I don't use them specifically. I may get to one or two of them in my own roundabout way."

"You are a golfer, right, Jerry?" He nods, so I continue. "How often do you practice and work on your swing, Jerry?"

"Oh, I'm always working on my swing. The driving range once a month. Out on the course, when I get to play, that is."

"The swing is basic. You swing that club all the time, constantly working to improve your performance. These five questions are your swing, Jerry. You use them specifically, in all their different forms. You never leave them out, because leaving them out would be like kicking the ball instead of swinging with the club. Does that make sense?"

"I see what you mean, Max."

"Look, the concepts are simple and there are obstacles in putting them to work. The first is that old habits die hard. The second is that learning a new way of thinking takes commitment and practice. The third is that your old behavior was satisfying some need. So using these tools may be uncomfortable at first. These are simple tools and it takes discipline to use them. And a shift in thinking. You always need the basics."

"What kind of shift in thinking, Max?"

"Many of us high-level managers are boss managers. We get in the habit of telling people what to do. We don't find out what our people want and how that ties in with what we want. We say, 'Jane, do X, Y, and Z.' If we asked Jane to self-evaluate, determine on her own what course of action she will take, she would learn how to do her own thinking. Jane would find her own solutions and perceive that we trust her.

"But we are always in a hurry so we do not take the time to guide Jane through her self-evaluation. She does not learn, and we end up solving the same problems over and over again, rather than taking care of them once. We have to shift from boss management to Lead Management.

"If you give a man a fish, he can feed himself for a day. If you teach him how to find the bait, put it on the hook, and toss the line in the right place, he can feed himself forever."

5

Repeat That, Please

Mental models . . . shape how we act.

—Peter Senge, *The Fifth Discipline*

OK, Max. Explain the details of the system one more time so I have a complete picture."

"Sure, Jerry. Repetition is part of the learning process."

I point to the diagram on the white board as I repeat my description of our model of human thought and action, the Triangle of Choice.

"We receive information through our senses and combine that information with what we already know into a perception, a picture of our current reality. We are constantly comparing what we perceive with what we want. If there is a match, we may ignore the situation or we may continue to act the way we are already acting.

"If there is a difference and that difference is important to us, we recognize it as a gap between what we want and what we perceive we have. Then we take

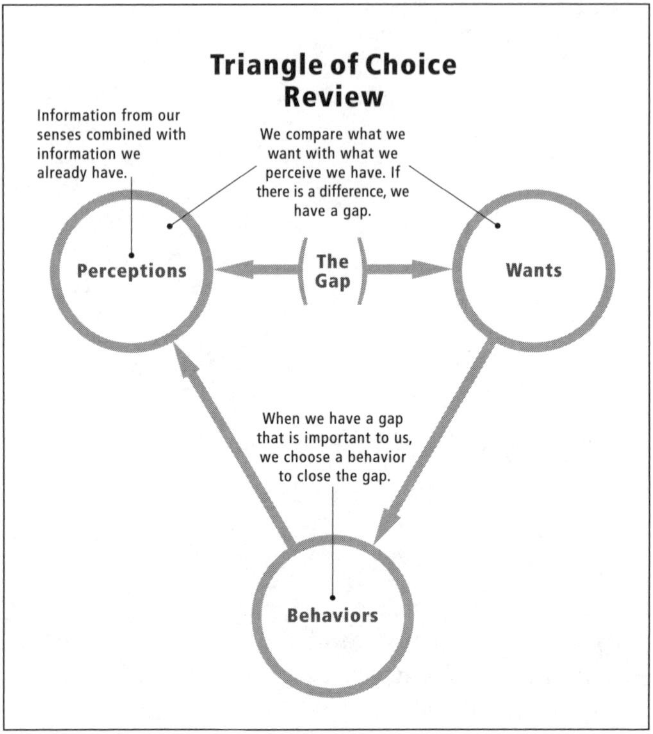

action in the form of behavior and attempt to close the gap.

"This model is at work in our minds and bodies twenty-four hours a day. When we wake up in the morning to a ringing alarm clock, we are faced with a gap. The alarm is ringing and we want the sound to stop. It is a gap between what we have and what we want. We choose a behavior, reaching over to turn off the alarm clock. It is a closed loop system. Everything we think, feel, sense, and do is connected to this model."

"Max, it sounds like we have a lot of choices. Am I right?"

"Yes, Jerry. We can choose what we perceive and how we interpret it. We can choose what we want, then change our minds and want the opposite. We can choose our behavior and then adjust it as we get feedback from our perceptions. All human beings are designed this way. They operate from the Triangle of Choice. Most people don't realize they have all these choices.

"The most effective people learn to operate consciously from a mental model of this process. They may not have it organized as formally as we do, but when they are looking at their own behaviors or alternatives, they are self-evaluating what goes on in this model, in their thoughts and actions."

"So if I can understand what's going on for me in my Triangle of Choice, I can make better choices. How do I do that, Max?"

"The Procedures That Lead to Change are one set of tools we apply to operate the system. When we ask ourselves, What do I want? we are looking at the strongest motivational force in the universe. Gravity wants to hold us to the earth. Our bodies want oxygen, so we breathe. We want food, so we eat. We want to satisfy our division managers, so we go to their meetings even though they are not effective. We are wanting something every minute of the day. Every choice we make is motivated by something we want."

"You mean that everything starts with what we want?"

"We always come back to what we want to make a choice, even if it is an unconscious habit.

"We receive information through our senses that we combine with what we already know to form our perceptions. We are constantly receiving information from people, events, and objects every second of our lives.

When we ask ourselves, Is this working? we are actually asking, What is the information I have received and how does it compare with what I want? Am I getting the results or is there a gap?"

"So there is a continuous process of receiving information and comparing it to what we want?" Jerry asks.

"Yes. And most of us stop with the first solution or answer we find. We try to close the gap too soon. We ask, What can I do? What behavior can I choose to get what I want? And when we come to the first solution, we jump to the doing.

"Using this model we want to evaluate what we are already doing. We want to continue or improve what is working and stop doing what is not working. In some situations we choose to do something else, exploring other possibilities and asking, What else can I do? This question generates alternatives. We may ask it many times until we have found all the alternatives that seem possible or one that seems to satisfy our needs in the best way.

"After we generate many alternatives, we ask which is most effective for achieving what we want. We take a strategic approach instead of a reactive approach. Rather than rushing to close the gap, we evaluate our choices against the desired results.

"We may leave the questions overnight and come back to them the next day with a new insight. The key here is to slow down the process, unless we are under a deadline. We hang out in the first four questions before we make a plan. We ask them repeatedly in many ways until we generate the right alternatives."

"Can you give me an example, Max?"

"Sure. When we were looking at your alternatives to create more time for yourself, you generated several possibilities. They included not going to the meeting and giving feedback from the minutes. You considered listening in on the telephone so you could work at your desk on other things when the meeting was in progress. You looked at not participating at all. You evaluated each of these alternatives, and then you rejected them, choosing to send other people in your place."

"Max, you said something about the right alternative and a plan. What is the difference between the right alternative and making the plan? As we look at alternatives, don't we usually weed out the bad ones and hone in on the good ones, the action that will get us what we want?"

"Yes, we do. And we often leave it at that. Through a process of elimination and other evaluations, we come down to a single choice. Then we go into action or just leave it hanging.

"When we ask ourselves, What will I do? we are formally closing the exploration and moving to a plan of action. Many people explore the alternatives and just assume that an action will take place. Making a plan that includes some parameters and details like deadlines and specific actions is the equivalent of making an agreement with ourselves.

"Jerry, when we were exploring possibilities for tomorrow's meetings, you eliminated several alternatives before making the final choice. But you did not commit to any action until I asked, 'What are you actually going to do?'"

"You mean I made a decision, but I did not commit to the action steps until you asked the question?"

"That's right, Jerry. When someone makes a decision, that does not mean they have made a commitment. When they make a plan and commit to it, then you can hold them accountable for the result. Without the agreement, without the specifics, there is nothing to be accountable for.

"When we lead others, we can ask the questions to get to the plan. In the end, we want a plan and agreements in most of what we do with ourselves and others so there is accountability. Lead Management drives accountability. It is based on making, keeping, and renegotiating clear agreements."

"It sounds like this takes a very conscious effort. You have to be deliberate in using this system until it becomes part of your way of thinking about everything. What you're describing is actually a way of life, Max."

"Yes, it is, Jerry. Once you start using the Triangle of Choice in your business dealings, you will find applications for it in every part of your life, in business, and with your family and friends. It is an effective tool for interacting with people in every situation."

6

What Do You Control?

The perception that someone "up there" is in control is based on an illusion — the illusion that anyone could master the dynamic and detailed complexity of an organization from the top.

—Peter Senge, *The Fifth Discipline*

Earlier, Jerry, you mentioned that you didn't want to attend Arthur's meetings. You called them *his* meetings."

"Yes, they're a waste of time. They make me angry and I have no control over what goes on in them."

"If the meetings produced what you wanted, what would they look like?"

"We would work from an agenda, at least some of the time. The meetings would have a specific business purpose. We would make agreements and then hold each other accountable for those agreements at future meetings."

"What have you tried to make this happen?"

Jerry moved his head from side to side, his face contorting.

"Long ago I suggested that we make some agreements, but on that day no one was interested. Arthur avoids confrontation, so I don't like to push back."

"Did that work for you? Are you getting what you want?"

"I said I wasn't." Abrupt. "It didn't work."

"You asked once and then you quit. Is that the kind of team player you want to be?"

"Whoa, there, Max. Do you think I am to blame for the lousy meetings?"

"First of all, I do not want to blame anyone. I do want to help you find alternatives. What else did you try?"

"I gave up. I didn't try anything else. But that's the way Arthur is."

"Do you want to work with people to have effective meetings?"

"Of course, I do." He pauses. "But, I don't want to invest my time and get no result."

"Would you like to have effective meetings with Arthur, even though he does not like confrontation?"

"Yes."

"Jerry, given that Arthur is the way he is, are there other things you could do to make the meetings more useful to you?"

"I could be stronger. But they're Arthur's meetings."

"That's an interesting point of view: Arthur's meetings. I have a different frame of reference. Do you want to hear it?"

"That's what I'm here for," throwing up his hands.

I ignore the sarcasm in his voice. "I believe that whenever you go to a meeting, it is your meeting, too."

"What do you mean, it's my meeting?"

"The meeting doesn't belong to the person who called it. All meetings need participants. Every person is responsible for the quality of the meeting if they agree to come. If you do not like the way the meeting is run or you find the results unacceptable, then you have the obligation to suggest alternatives and lead others toward improvements. If you are not willing to live up to that obligation, then do not complain about how it works."

"You know, whenever we finish one of these meetings with Arthur, we come out shaking our heads. We talk in the hall and in the elevator about what a waste of time it was."

"Jerry, who is we?"

"Oh. The other managers. We share our reactions."

"Ah, the meeting after the meeting. Does this create results for you, Jerry? Talking behind Arthur's back?"

"No, it doesn't. But I don't want to confront him in the meeting."

"Is confrontation your only option?"

He thinks for a minute or two and scribbles some notes on a pad. "I can do it offline. I can volunteer to lead part of the meeting. Demonstrate how we can be more effective. I could explain how I would like the meetings to work. Tell Arthur what I want."

"Would one or all of these alternatives help you partner with Arthur?"

"I'm not sure, but it is worth a try."

"That would be a great start. Is there anything else you can think of?"

"I can ask for some agreements in the meetings and make commitments myself so that others can see the value in it."

"These are all things you can do. What will you do?"

"I'll do all of them."

"Do you remember the four things you said you can do?"

"Yes, I wrote them down, except the last one." Jerry made additional notes as he spoke. "I'll talk to Arthur offline, tell him what I want, and offer to lead a portion of the next meeting I attend. In that part of the meeting, I will lead people to discuss alternatives to how we can make our meetings more productive, and then I will make specific agreements that I will live up to."

"When will you do this, Jerry?"

"Before and during the next meeting I attend with Arthur."

"Excellent work. What did you learn from this self-evaluation and my questions?"

"Is this a test?" he asks in a loud voice.

"No. I want you to continue to use the Procedures That Lead to Change to look at your thinking and behaviors. I can assist you by asking you questions to help you self-evaluate. When I ask you what you've learned, I am asking you to share your perceptions of what we've been talking about."

"I guess I get your point, Max — this whole business about whose meeting it is. When I criticize without making a persistent effort to change the situation, then I am as responsible for the lack of results from these meetings as every other participant. It just feels like I have no control."

"What *can* you control, Jerry?"

I can hear the clock ticking on the wall. The sun shines through the window and the dust in the room twinkles in the light. Jerry plays with a pencil as he thinks about his next answer.

"Lord knows, I've tried to control everyone and

everything around me: my kids, my wife, the people who work for me, with me, and above me. I've never been able to control any of them. Sometimes I can get a response and often I cannot even do that. Most things that occur in this world are beyond my control."

"That is very perceptive. Here is a simple diagram that shows how little we control. We call the concept the Microdot of Control. I'll show you what I mean."

I draw the diagram on a piece of paper and stand next to Jerry at his desk as I explain it.

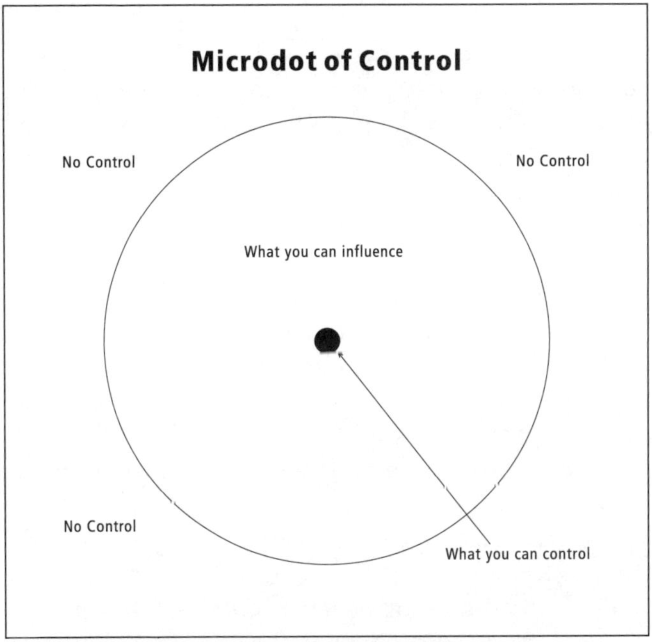

"What falls in the dot in the center is what we can control. What falls within the circle is what we can influence. What's left outside the circle we cannot control or influence at all. What do you notice about the diagram?"

"The small dot in the middle — what we can control — it is tiny compared to what we can influence. Most of the world is outside the circle and outside our control and influence as well."

"That's true, Jerry. So what can you control?"

"I guess it boils down to just my very insignificant self. I can only control me. And even then, I feel out of control at times."

"If you can only control yourself, then what can other people do?"

"They can't do any more than I can. They can control themselves and maybe have some influence on other things, events, and people. That's why this whole self-evaluation thing is important. If we can only control ourselves, then why do we spend so much time trying to control others?"

"When you are trying to control other people, Jerry, what is your motivation?"

"I want something. When I go to the staff meeting and I fail to participate, I want to avoid frustration and the rejection of my ideas. I want other people to do what I want them to do."

"Are there other things you want when you are in an unproductive meeting?"

"Maybe. Part of it is that I don't want to be associated with the failure of the meetings so I can walk away and say I had nothing to do with it. I did not participate; therefore, what happens as a result of the meeting is not my fault. Not very effective thinking, is it, Max?"

"Well, it is effective for avoiding responsibility and being comfortable in the moment. It is ineffective for creating a productive meeting."

"I want opposite things at the same time. On the positive side, I want to have extremely productive meetings. On the negative side, since I have not seen a way to control the situation, I want to be uninvolved. But I always want something, and I choose, as you would say, my behaviors based on what I want in the moment."

7

You Make the Choice

Not being able to control events,
I control myself, and I adapt myself to them,
if they do not adapt themselves to me.

—Michel de Montaigne

I may not have control, but I still have influence. I can see that Arthur's behavior in the meeting, the way he leads, has controlled my response, and I don't want anyone doing that to me."

"Jerry, I'm glad you brought that up, because it leads us to another critical point. Something called Locus of Control. People who think that they have no control over events and situations, people who are victims of what happens around them, have an external Locus of Control. They believe they are controlled by external events and other people.

"People who believe that they always have alternatives in the way they respond to events and other people, regardless of the circumstances, have an internal Locus of Control. They know that external events influence them, but do not control their choices. They know they can choose different approaches to deal with events they cannot control.

"When you say Arthur's behavior controlled your response, how did he do that?"

"He's the boss. I have to be nice to him, do things his way, otherwise I'll lose my job."

"What is your evidence? How many people lost their jobs in the last two years when they disagreed with Arthur or suggested to him an alternative way of doing something?"

"I can't think of any. So I exaggerated, Max."

"Didn't you make the choice to respond the way you have in the past?"

"Not consciously. I didn't sit down and decide that I would not participate. That plan kind of evolved."

"Could you have chosen other ways of approaching Arthur's behavior?"

"I just did. I could have taken other actions like the ones I just planned with you a few minutes ago."

"When you chose those alternatives, did Arthur control your choice?"

"No, you led me to self-evaluate."

"Are you going to give Arthur credit for your new plan, Jerry?"

"No, he doesn't know about it and he wasn't involved in the new plan."

"Then why do you want to blame him for your previous choice, the one that evolved, as you said, because his leadership controlled your response? If he was in control of your ineffective response, why don't you give him credit for your plan, for the effective response? Isn't your new response a reaction to his behavior?"

Jerry takes a deep breath, grabs the coffee cup on his

desk, and stands up, crossing the room toward the door. "That is a hard question, Max. You want some?" he asks, lifting the cup in the air. "I need to think about it before I answer."

"None for me, Jerry."

"I'll be back in a minute," he says as he leaves the room.

People often do that when they feel cornered: reach for the coffee, make a phone call, divert the conversation. Jerry needs time to think this out.

I notice something else about the words Jerry chose to describe what he wanted. He talked about wanting to avoid situations. Avoidance is not a good strategy for a sales manager.

When Jerry returns to the room, he is visibly agitated. I am sitting in the deep leather chair and he stands over me, his cup waving in his hand, drops of coffee spilling over the side.

"What he does will influence me, Max. I do not live in a vacuum. People are doing things around me all the time and I have to react to what they do."

"Yes, that's true, Jerry. And, you are leaving out an important part of this. Take a look at the Triangle of Choice. Who chooses what you want? Who chooses what your perceptions mean? Who chooses your behavior?"

"I do, but I am influenced by what Arthur does."

"Right! You do not control what Arthur does. Once Arthur chooses his behavior, then you are influenced to make a choice. You control the choice you make.

"And whose choice is it to be influenced, Jerry?"

"If I ignore him, he'll be upset."

"Is ignoring him the only alternative?"

"OK, OK. There are alternatives."

"That's the point, Jerry. Arthur's actions create a situation where you must make a choice. The choice you make is your own. You choose how you respond. Arthur does not choose your response."

"As I said, I just did that with my new plan. I could have chosen that plan earlier. There may even be other responses I have not thought of yet. So what are you saying, Max?"

"It goes back to what I said earlier. You can always change your perceptions, change what you want, or change your behavior. The actions of others create moments of choice. No one controls your response. You make any choice you want. You have to deal with the consequences of your choices, but that has to do with what you are willing to accept. Again, it has to do with what you want.

"If you say that Arthur controls your response, then you are operating from an external Locus of Control. You are saying that he controls your choices. If he has that much control over you, why don't you love his meetings? Can't he control your likes and dislikes as well?"

"You're getting a little sarcastic, Max."

"Sorry, Jerry. I am just making a point. If you say that you will consider what Arthur does in the response you choose and you have control over the decision, then you are operating from an internal Locus of Control. You are behaving like you have control over your choices. Who does control your choices, Jerry?"

"I do."

"Even when the choice is a habit?" He turns and walks behind his desk and falls into the chair, looking exhausted. He sips coffee, staring over the top of the cup at me.

"Yes, Max." He looks at the Triangle of Choice on

the white board. "Ultimately, I control the meaning of what I perceive, I choose what I want, and I choose my behaviors. This is all a little frightening and very powerful at the same time."

"I'm glad you see that. Once you accept the fact that you are always in control of what you perceive, what you want, and what you do, you have a huge responsibility. You are now accountable for the meaning you place on the information you receive, for what you want, and the behaviors you choose to get what you want. You are always choosing, whether you do it consciously or unconsciously. You are in control of you."

"It sounds like I can't blame anyone else for the outcomes I produce. Is that what you're saying, Max?"

"That is true, Jerry. People are going to do things. Events will occur. In essence, whatever happens outside your mind is information. You get to choose what that information means, what importance you place on your perceptions of that information, and how it fits with what you already know.

"Then you compare it with what you want. If you want something different, you will choose a behavior to close the gap between what you want and what you perceive you have."

Jerry replies, "So I observe the lack of an agenda, random repeated communication, and no agreements, and I decide that the meetings Arthur leads are ineffective. I can continue to make little or no contribution as I have in the past or I can choose another course of action.

"I will choose based on what I want most: my momentary comfort or productive meetings, creativity or suffering in silence."

"Yes, Jerry. And you've committed to four things you will do."

"It sounds great in the case of the meetings Arthur leads, but what about other situations? I had a major account salesman quit last week. He was working on a big new customer for six months. We were supposed to close the deal next week and now this guy is gone. He really screwed us."

"What do you mean by screwed you?"

"Well, he had the relationships. We paid him to build them. Now we may have to start over, or somehow work our way into the buyer's good graces without losing the momentum."

"That kind of language, 'He really screwed us,' is very external. Like a mysterious force, this salesman controls your future. Did he say anything negative to the prospect that would hurt your chances of getting the account?"

"No, not that I know of. The salesman actually told the prospect he was leaving before he even told us, and assured the buyer that we would live up to the commitments he made."

"What do you mean by screwed you, then?"

"Well, I guess he didn't exactly screw us. He left for a great opportunity: a management position. He was taking care of himself. He really did not do anything but leave. I guess that is the information I have to deal with. I don't want to turn it into something it's not. Now I get to choose how I will deal with the situation and the prospect."

"Great, Jerry. That thinking comes from an internal Locus of Control. Something happened and now you deal with it rather than say that someone did something to you and now you are a victim."

"I guess I took it personally. I invested a lot of time in this guy and then he left. Maybe I should be proud that he learned so much on this job that he was able to get a better one." Jerry smiles. "I wished him luck, anyway."

"Jerry, we tend to judge people. We are judging machines and that will never stop. If we did not use our judgment, we would fail much more often. Whenever we make a choice, we are using our judgment.

"When I am upset by what others do, I try to keep in mind that they are not usually doing it to hurt me. In most cases they are doing what they think is best for them and have not even considered how it will impact me at all. How I choose to deal with the consequences of that person's actions and lack of consideration is up to me. I have control over what is next.

"I want to add one more thing to this part of our conversation, Jerry. Earlier, when I asked what you wanted in the meetings that Arthur leads, you implied and specifically indicated that you wanted to avoid certain things. Do you remember?"

"Oh, yes. I want to avoid frustration and the rejection." He holds up his hand to stop my next question.

"I know. I know. Avoidance does not work. I coach my salespeople on that all the time. You can move toward something or away from it. When you are avoiding, you are moving away, and in most circumstances, especially where you want to influence someone, you need to move ahead with your ideas. I get it. But I'm not yet living what I preach in all cases. Most of the time I'm aware of it, Max."

"That's the best any of us can do, Jerry. What I am introducing you to is a practice: the practice of Lead Management. It is just what the term implies: you keep practicing for continuous improvement. Getting closer and closer to perfection, but never getting there. We are human beings and we need to have a little compassion for our foibles and the failures of others, too.

"One of the key principles of Lead Management is that people are always doing the best they can to get what they want at any given moment. They may have the skills and knowledge to do better, but their habits get in the way. Yours, mine, and everyone's."

8

Choosing Your Behaviors

All we do is behave from birth to death.

—Dr. William Glasser

Let's go back to Arthur again, for a moment. You said the meetings he leads are ineffective. Did you tell him that?"

"Yes, I did, Max. He was angry that I was critical of his meetings — excuse me — of the meetings he leads. Does that kind of comment indicate something about my Locus of Control?"

"Not as much as it says something about your judgments. In your opinion, the meetings Arthur leads may be ineffective, but you described them in another way earlier that was more accurate. You said they did not lead to agreements and accountability. Those are not judgments. You are reporting what actually happens or does not happen in the meetings.

"That is the difference between criticism and feedback. Criticism places a value judgment on the situation or event. Feedback reports what happened or what was left out.

"Did you ask Arthur if he wanted feedback?"

"No, I did not. I just told him what I thought one day in the hallway after one of the meetings. I don't blame him for his reaction."

"Do you have any idea what criteria Arthur has for a quality meeting, Jerry?"

"I don't know. His meetings don't lead to anything of value that I can see, so he may have no criteria."

"Is that what Arthur wants?"

"I don't know what Arthur wants. I never asked."

I let the answer sit in the silence of the room for a time. "In this model of human behavior, it is important to find out what the other person wants. When you give people your criticism without finding out what they want first, it is not feedback. Especially if you do not have a cooperative relationship.

"Did you have any evidence that Arthur wanted your feedback?"

"No, he didn't ask for it and I didn't ask him if he wanted it."

"Do you like having people share their negative judgments of you without asking you first?"

"No."

"Why would Arthur be any different?"

"OK, I was critical, but he frustrates me."

"What does he do that you choose to get frustrated over?"

"Hold it, Max. You think I choose frustration. You mean that frustration is a choice? Like something I can control?"

"Yes and no. When you get a feeling of frustration, you have no direct control over the feeling. But a feeling is only a signal. You do have a choice as to how you respond to the signal.

"Feelings are part of what we call Total Behavior. Feelings do not happen in isolation. Whenever a feeling arises, you are also doing something and thinking something at the same time. And you have sensations in your body like a rapid heartbeat or sweaty palms. We refer to the body sensations as physiology.

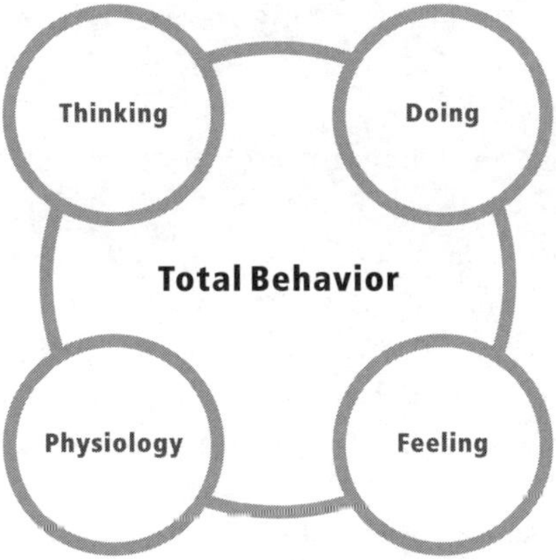

"Every behavior is made up of these four components: thinking, doing, physiology, feeling. We call this Total Behavior because one component does not exist without the others.

"We say we are feeling frustrated, and frustration is part of a Total Behavior. We identify the behavior by the strongest signal. There is a definite thought, action, and body sensation that happens at the same time as that feeling of frustration."

"OK, Max. But I remember that you said we can choose our behaviors. I can't tell myself what feelings to have. They just spring up. And I can't necessarily change my physiology by sheer will."

"That is true, Jerry. You cannot directly control your feelings or your physiology. What can you control?"

"I can control what I think and what I do. That is what I'm responsible for."

"Can your thinking change your feelings?"

"Maybe not as soon as the feeling arises, but if I change what I am thinking about or the way I am thinking, it may have some influence on my feelings and my physiology."

"What about what you are doing? What effect does it have?"

"I suppose the same."

"Right, Jerry. We can directly control our thinking and what we are doing, like speaking, listening, moving, or sitting still. We can control our feelings and physiology indirectly, by changing what we think and do."

"You're saying that after I get the initial signal of frustration, it is my responsibility to choose the actions and thoughts that will terminate the signal. If I accept the ongoing frustration as being a choice, it must mean I am coming from an internal Locus of Control. I get to choose and maybe make the frustration go away. Are you saying that Arthur's actions are not causing my frustration?"

"Yes and no. Arthur does what he does, without concern for you or not noticing how it affects you. You get a signal of frustration. Then you choose how you will behave in regard to what he does.

"You can sit in the meetings he leads and do nothing. You can participate in a way that leads Arthur and others to self-evaluate. You can choose to frustrate or you can change your thoughts and take some action to influence the process.

"You have already changed one thought, Jerry. When we first started this morning, you said these meetings were Arthur's meetings. How do you think of them now?"

"What you said. It's my meeting as well as Arthur's."

"Let's try something. Describe what is happening in your mind and body when you are frustrated with Arthur's actions. When you are in one of these meetings, what are you thinking?"

"I'm usually thinking, Can't we move on? What is all this about anyway? These meetings never lead to anything. I can't sit here another minute. Where's the coffee?"

"In those moments, what are you doing, Jerry?"

"I am usually doodling on a pad. Squirming in my chair. Moving my legs. Looking down. Drinking coffee. Trying to turn off the noise, the conversation. Maybe work on something else."

"And you are feeling frustrated. Are you feeling anything else?"

"Oh, yeah. I'm feeling pissed."

"What is going on in your body, with your physiology?"

"I feel tension in my neck. My legs are tight. I am hardly breathing. I want to get up and scream. I am uptight."

"Do you see that you are able to describe this Total Behavior, all four components, Jerry?"

"Yes. As I was describing it, I was starting to relive some of that frustration. This is interesting information, but what can I do with it, Max? I don't think I need practice being frustrated." He laughs. "Do you think that reliving this will change it?"

"Jerry, if you can recreate the experience of frustration just by describing it in terms of Total Behavior, then maybe you can design a new Total Behavior to replace it. Do you want to be frustrated?"

"No."

"What do you want instead?"

"I want to be creative around this feeling. Just treat it like... the signal that it is. I want it to go away and I want to substitute something else more powerful. To use the term you used earlier, I don't want to feel like a victim. I want to come from an internal Locus of Control. Like, I'm in charge here. What do I do to design a new behavior?"

"You've already taken some steps. Remember your plan? The four things you said you would do? That's part of it."

Jerry nods his head affirmatively.

I go on. "Let's try the new behavior. You've said what you want. You do not have what you want now. What would you be doing if you were acting more... creatively, if you were coming from an internal Locus of Control?"

"I would be sitting still, listening, and speaking when I wanted to add to or redirect the conversation. I would be taking notes instead of doodling, and I would be watching the actions and reactions of others around the room. I would be asking questions of others to get them to self-evaluate."

"That is great, Jerry. What would you be thinking?"

"I would be thinking about the issues, focusing on what people are saying, and asking, How can I contribute to this meeting, since it is my meeting, too? I would be asking questions of myself to evaluate my own actions in the group."

"What will be going on in your body and what feelings might you have?"

"I will be calm, relaxed, very loose. I will feel powerful, engaged, rather than acting out my frustration."

"Good job, Jerry."

"This all sounds easier said than done, Max. As I describe this Total Behavior, I can see that it is a little like a practice session. I do feel calmer and somewhat more relaxed."

"Jerry, none of this will happen overnight. If you want to lead from the Triangle of Choice and practice Lead Management, you will have to work on it. Within weeks you can integrate these ideas into your leadership style. With the methods of self-evaluation I am going to teach you to use, you will be able to change and improve many things in your work and personal life. It is up to you.

"The company pays me to provide coaching to people at your level. Do you want my coaching? We can talk on the phone for an hour each week. You're a quick study. With my help, you will be up to speed in no time."

"Yes, Max. I do want your help."

"Of course, it's only if you want to do this. If you choose to commit."

"Do I have a choice? Don't answer that question, Max. Of course, I have a choice. I always have a choice. And this is something I want to learn, how to use this model. I'm willing to commit to the coaching. Before you leave, let's schedule some dates."

"I'm glad you are making that commitment, Jerry."

"Look, Max, although I have some trepidation, I am excited by what we've done here today. I will do whatever it takes to make the meetings I attend more productive."

"Jerry, I think that life as you know it is now over.

As you gain experience using Lead Management, you will see glaring and shocking examples of boss managers who do great damage as they lead. In some cases, these leaders will be producing extraordinary results. The results will be at a huge cost to their organizations and their people.

"Such organizations are often demoralized, sapped of their most valuable strengths and creativity, and diverted from even greater results. Led by leaders who are feeding their egos, who do not have the discipline to make deliberate choices, these organizations fail to maximize their greatest asset, their people. In this kind of atmosphere, most people fail to grow, fail to improve their skills, and fail to take ownership for the results they create. They are stuck at the same level of performance, year after year, waiting to be told what to do next. Waiting for retirement.

"You will see this more clearly than you've ever experienced it before. If you use the Lead Management model as your guide, you will lead and influence people to new levels of performance. Even when they do not participate with you, Lead Management will impact their world."

9

WE'RE IN IT TOGETHER

If I am not for you, who will I be?
If I am not for you now, when will I be for anyone?
If I am not for you, who will be for me?
We are in it together.
Whether I like it or not.
This is the territory.

—JILL MORRIS

"Maybe you can help me with an issue I'm struggling with, Max."

"Sure, go for it. Tell me about the issue, Jerry."

"I ask all my regional managers to take on some of the administrative and planning work of the division's sales effort. It gives them a bigger sense of the overall sales picture and they also learn a lot about what is needed to move up in the organization. They act like my board of directors."

"That seems like a good idea, Jerry. It creates a much higher level of participation than you would find in most sales organizations."

"Yes, it does, when it works. I have one regional manager who agrees to take on specific assignments and then leaves them until the last minute, usually until I have to complete them myself. I would object, however, he is my most productive guy, a man who has broken every sales goal and previous record each quarter for the last three years."

"What does he say about not getting the work done, not living up to what he's agreed to do?"

"He always has a reasonable excuse: new salespeople to train, new customers to meet, out saving an order. But I still want him to live up to his commitments to me. Otherwise, there's a credibility gap. I don't know what to believe."

"Does he lie to you, Jerry?"

"No, Max, it is more a matter of optimism. He is a guy who truly believes he can do something when he commits to it, and then he goes with his priorities and can't deliver everything he's promised. He means well and he falls short in this one area.

"I've thought of not asking him to participate in the process, in planning and working with the other regional managers, but that is not fair to him or to them. We lose the value of Sal's very important input, and we need his experience to make the whole organization grow, not just his region.

"The projects I ask Sal to take on, that he agrees to take on, will help him get a big boost in his performance. It would be good for him, too."

"Jerry, what you are saying is that you do for Sal what he should be doing for himself. Is that true? You take on his work, the work he agreed to do. At the last minute, you complete the work for him. Is he capable of doing the work he agrees to do?"

"Oh yes. He can do it. When he does the things I ask

him to do for his own use, he turns out perfect results, on time and in a very presentable manner.

"Just the other day I asked Sal to put together projections from his territory for the potential sales of a new product he's been asking for. He delivered them on time.

"But the week before, I asked for specific information from him that would add to the design of a new reporting system and would help the company be more accurate in its forecasting. He never delivered, even though he promised to do it. He probably couldn't see the impact on his customers.

"I ended up digging for the information myself on the night before it was due. I didn't get out of here until 8:00 P.M."

"Do you get the downside of letting him off the hook?"

"I think I do, Max. First of all, when I let him get away with not delivering what he promised, I am saying it is OK to do that. He probably feels that he can do whatever he likes in regard to his commitments, as long as he brings in more business.

"Secondly, he probably has less respect for me when I let him get away with it over and over."

"Are there other negative impacts in what you are doing when you do for Sal what he should be doing himself?"

"I let him off the hook. I think he learns the wrong lessons — that he can get away with anything."

"There is another side to it, Jerry. You rob him of the opportunity to learn from the experience of having to complete the assignments. He also fails to gain the knowledge he would get from doing his own research and planning. Do you see that?"

"Yes, I do now."

"Anything else you see happening?"

"Well, I get pissed off. I am not doing the work I want to be doing. Sometimes I single him out in a meeting, try to embarrass him; make casual, off-the-cuff remarks about his failure to deliver. It seems counterproductive."

"That is part of what we call the Do For/Do To loop, Jerry. First we do for the other person what they should be doing for themselves, and then we do it to them to get revenge, to embarrass or shame them into doing what they said they would do. Next, we are embarrassed or feel bad about what we did and we go back to Doing For. It is a continuous loop that we choose in the moment."

"Sounds right to me, Max. I'm caught in this loop with Sal and other people all the time. I really like the guy and respect his strengths. And, I'm getting dizzy going around and around in this loop."

"How long have you been choosing to keep this system going, Jerry?"

Do For / Do To Loop

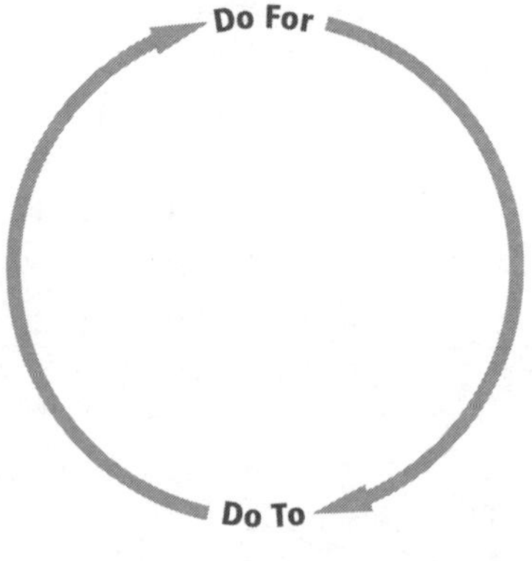

"Stop right there. Are you saying I am choosing this?"

"Don't you have a choice?"

"I want to keep him happy and producing. So I look the other way on this issue. I've been doing it for two years. I guess he expects me to step in whenever he fails to deliver on his commitments. At least in this context."

"That's a big part of the downside of Do For. After a while, the other people not only expect it, but they feel entitled to have you step in to save the day, and they are right. You set up the expectation, and when you get angry and don't step in, then you are doing it to them. You've supported the entitlement and now that's what you can expect."

"What's the solution, Max? I want to end this sickness now."

"We have a name for the solution, Jerry. We call it Do With."

"Another concept, Max?"

"Yes, another one, Jerry. Do With encompasses all that we have talked about and much more.

"Do With is the only way I know to break the Do For/Do To cycle. It is a combination of actions we can take and an attitude we adopt to work with other people. When people in an organization act from the posture of Do With, they are creating a cohesive force that will move people to new highs in performance."

I pull a sheet of paper out of my bag and hand it to Jerry. It contains the definitions of Do With and Responsibility. "Read this page and tell me what you notice."

The page says:

> Do With is taking responsibility for what you
> want, respecting others and what they want,

> and supporting them to take responsibility for what they want.
>
> In this definition, responsibility is learning to choose effective behaviors to get what you want and be the person you want to be, while you assist others to learn to choose effective behaviors to get what they want and be the people they want to be.

"What stands out for you about this definition, Jerry?"

"It seems to indicate that both Do With and responsibility are ongoing processes of learning and support for others that begin with knowing what you want."

"That is one of the best summations I've ever heard, Jerry."

"Great, but how do you do it, Max? It's one thing to have goals like support, learning and knowing what you want all the time. It's another to live these concepts. To make them real."

"I'm glad you see that, Jerry. Let's look at your situation with Sal, as an example. There are several things you could do to lead him toward Do With."

"What would that look like, Max?"

"First, you have to get a handle on what you want and what you're willing to do to get it."

"Starting there again, what I want. Should we do this now, Max?"

"Yes. Take a few minutes to think it over."

Jerry looks to the ceiling for his answer, and after a while he scratches his neck and starts talking. "I want to support Sal to live up to his agreements or have him tell me up front that he doesn't want to do what I ask."

"That would be a start. What else could you do?"

"Something about learning. Like we are in this

together and we have to figure out how to do this Do With thing. Maybe we fail sometimes, but we learn from our mistakes. It won't be perfect, but we can lead each other through some self-evaluations. Ask those questions. What did you call them?"

"The Procedures That Lead to Change."

"Yeah, the Procedures. Anyway, I need to get pretty proficient in asking the questions, navigating the model, so I can teach my people. Lead by example. I am looking forward to your coaching.

"I need to cop to my share in creating this Do For / Do To loop. How I keep it going, as well. Explain the negative impacts of Do For in detail."

"Jerry, that is a critical part of Lead Management and Do With. If you do some self-evaluating in public with your people, individually and in groups, you will be making self-disclosures that give them a greater sense of your own struggles and humanity. It will lead them to be honest with you.

"When you reveal your imperfections, they will be more willing to reveal their vulnerabilities, too. You are not only saying we are in this together, you are modeling the process. You lead others to self-evaluate through your own self-evaluation. That is Do With."

"I guess I'll tell Sal that I won't do his assignments for him anymore. Break the pattern for his sake and mine. I can't change the rules without giving him notice."

"So that leads him to the point where he needs to make a commitment. What is the next step, Jerry?"

"I'll ask him what he wants, given these changed conditions. Also, what he is willing to do to get what he wants; what is he doing to get it; does he think it will work; what are the alternatives. Lead him using the Procedures That Lead to Change. Wander around in his answers and what you called the first four questions until we've explored a lot of alternatives. Then ask him to commit to a plan."

"What will happen if he does not want to commit or he has a problem defining what he wants?"

"In the spirit of Do With, I will stay in the process with him. Keep on asking questions about what he does want. But I am not sure of where to go from there, Max. Is there part of the system I'm missing?"

"When you said 'in the spirit of Do With,' you were embodying one of the key elements of the system that does not appear in any diagram or map of the model. It is the question of who you want to be in this situation — a question you can be asking every moment of your life.

"We often shoot from the hip and go with the unconscious patterns of thinking and action that we have evolved over the years. We do the same old thing. Get angry, tell people what they should do, tell them what they have failed at. Most managers say this old way is faster and gets the same result."

Jerry says, "Do With looks like it takes much more time up front, but I imagine the benefits of it will result in tremendous savings in time and effort that last far into the future. Sounds like a good investment. But what does it really take, Max? What am I missing?"

"Jerry, to live from Do With, to bring this model into reality, you will have to change how you choose to be, who you want to be in any given moment. This means you change what you think and what you do, and along with it your feelings and physiology will change, too.

"Do you want to be a person who gets your way regardless of the impact of your actions on other people? Or do you want to get involved with others like they matter? Where both your needs and theirs are important?"

"My God. Before it was what do I want. Now it is who do I want to be. Is that it? It sounds like a huge commitment, Max. I'll bet not many people are willing to make that choice, as you might call it."

"You would be surprised. If leaders show their people, through their own actions, that they are willing to be vulnerable, to self-evaluate with others, to make and admit their mistakes, then people will follow. Not all, but a critical mass large enough to change the character of a group or an entire organization. And then others will follow when they see it working."

"You're saying that I have to come from the belief that the system works, this Triangle of Choice? I stick with the model, ask the questions, and do my own self-evaluation. Then Sal will follow and get to where I want him to go?

"But, if Sal will not choose what he wants or will not make a commitment, what do I do next, Max?"

"Let's look at the model for a moment. When Sal says he does not know what he wants, where else can you go?"

Jerry looks at the diagram on the board. "Perceptions and Behaviors. I want to know what he perceives in this situation. Does he understand what I want? What is it about what I want that is objectionable to him?

"If it is unclear to him, I can explain the needs of the organization and my need to have him comply with my request.

"Then I can ask, if he did what I want, what he perceives would happen.

"I can tell him that I'm open to alternatives.

"I won't rush the process. But I'll keep him on track. Help him stick to what is important.

"I'll come from the spirit of Do With, rather than doing it for him or to him; be someone who wants to create this atmosphere, this territory of Do With.

"And I need to get an agreement from him. I'm not going to give up until I have that agreement. One that he lives up to."

"I'm glad you see that, Jerry. If there is no specific, explicit agreement, there is nothing to hold him accountable for."

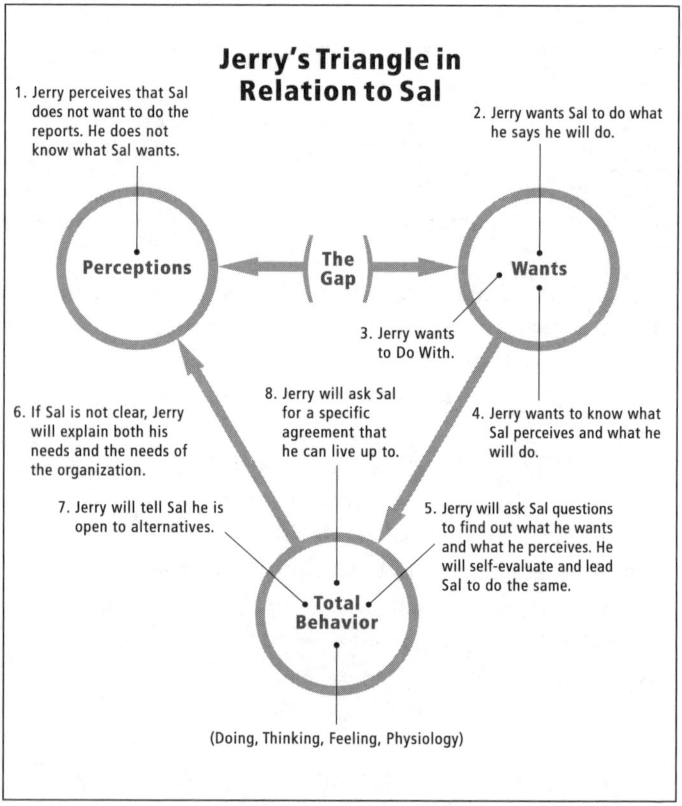

10

Did Anyone Make a Commitment?

Success on any major scale requires you to accept responsibility.

—Michael Korda

"What do you mean by specific and explicit, Max?"

"An agreement has specific deliverables, deadlines, and quality standards determined by all involved.

"Request an agreement from Sal. Ask him to deliver the next assignment on time, in the manner you've described. Be specific with dates and what you will expect from him in regard to other deliverables.

"Take the time to negotiate something that works for both of you and still achieves the goal."

"And I should ask him to tell me what we've agreed to at the end; check out his understanding?"

"Yes, that's right, Jerry. You may also give him the opportunity to turn down the assignment. If he does not like the first one, then have a second alternative.

"After he agrees to the assignment, you need to

negotiate some standards for reporting and follow-up. You have to include what I call an early warning system. Ask him to contact you one week before the assignment is due to tell you the status of his work and if he will meet the deadline.

"This is the beginning of Do With: setting clear parameters and getting solid agreements that include some form of check-in prior to the due date."

"You mean I should get progress reports from anyone I give an assignment to? That seems like a lot of follow-up to me, Max."

"The progress report can be as little as 'Jerry, I will have the assignment done on time' or 'Jerry, I am running behind and we have to renegotiate.' The progress report is more important than the due date."

"Why is that?"

"If Sal is on time, then you get your information and go on with your plans and actions. If Sal is going to be late, then you have to adjust your schedule and maybe the schedules of many others. You want to know about delays and changes as far in advance as you can. Most agreements people make should include a progress report.

"This process is important because accountability is based on the agreements you and other people make with each other. Can you hold the other person accountable for what you want if there is no agreement, Jerry?"

"I can try, but it probably will be hit and miss. That's a good part of why people fail to deliver on time or at the quality and level of detail that I expect."

"That's a valid observation, Jerry. You can hold people accountable only if they have explicitly agreed to deliver some result or have promised to behave in a specific manner.

"If there is just an implication of an agreement, you may leave critical parameters fuzzy and open to interpretation. Real business agreements are sealed with the words 'I agree,' or 'I promise to deliver X, Y, and Z.'"

"Under those terms, I have no agreements with any of my managers, Max. When we discuss a plan, we usually generate action items. People say they will take care of specific action items, but we never use the term 'agreement.' Now that I think of it, many of our action items are delivered late."

"You are not alone, Jerry. Last week, the top executive in one of the other business units told me that less than 30 percent of the things she thought she had agreements about were delivered on time, or in the manner she expected. She said that she and her people never used the words 'agree' or 'agreement' and that almost all the agreements made between her people were implied rather than specific. I think it is true in most organizations."

"Max, I've never tracked how many agreements are made with me and how many are kept. This brief discussion has me thinking that our performance record is not any more than 30 percent either. And I usually get no progress reports."

"Accountability is getting people to connect their choices of wants, perceptions, and behaviors with the results they produce, Jerry. It is taking ownership for the consequences of those choices in keeping or failing to keep our agreements with ourselves and with other people.

"By ownership, I mean we do not blame, deny, or defend what we've created through our own choices.

"In your organization, who is responsible for creating accountability?"

"I guess I am. I don't get clear, specific agreements,

and then I jump in if people fail to deliver the result. I do for them what they should be doing for themselves. I just let them off the hook and I take on more and more work. Now they expect me to do it all. I can't blame anyone else."

"What level of accountability do you want in your sales organization?"

"Of course, I want people to be accountable for the results they agree to produce. If they can't deliver, I want them to tell me they can't and I want them to renegotiate. I want to stop stepping in to rescue people, and I want my people to stop expecting me to do so."

"What can you do to get what you want, Jerry?"

"I can ask people to make specific agreements. I can help them self-evaluate when they fail to live up to those agreements. But I do not have to jump in and do it for them. I can lead them to see and experience the consequences of their choices. That would be a big step toward holding them accountable for the results they create."

"Under those circumstances, who would be responsible for creating accountability?"

"Everyone in my organization. I would expect others to hold me accountable for my agreements and results as well. I want other people to guide me in my self-evaluations. Make everyone a lead manager."

"That's the point of Lead Management, Jerry. Everyone is leading and managing. They are just leading and managing different things. We manage priorities, processes, and ourselves. We lead people if they allow us."

11

Shared Leadership

Great groups and great leaders create each other.

—Warren Bennis and Patricia Ward Biederman

"Max, all of this is great in theory. I'd like to see it work with a group of people. I have a meeting right after lunch that I'd like you to be in on. Do you have the time?"

"Yes, I do. What is it about?"

"We were supposed to ship an important order yesterday to our biggest customer, and it did not go out. New product, old story. The meeting is at 1:30 with Arthur, Tom Winston, the production manager, and Sidney Swift, our engineering manager. I'm to lead the meeting, but I would like you to step in wherever you think you can help."

"I will be happy to do that, Jerry. Under what circumstances do you want me to step in? What do you want to accomplish in the meeting? I want to get clear on my role and yours."

"I want the equipment delivered to our customer on

time. I would like to see you demonstrate how Lead Management works in a group. I'll ask you to lead us when I think it is necessary. And I'll contribute if I see something I can add. Is that OK with you, Max?"

"Yes, I will be happy to help."

We end our morning session to make phone calls and go to lunch.

We return from lunch an hour later and head for a conference room in the sales department. I'm introduced to two of the three other executives attending the meeting. Arthur and I go way back, so we exchange greetings.

Jerry frames up the situation. "We're here to discuss our failure to meet the shipping commitment last Friday on our first RF4900 test system to Milov Industries. I was told about the delay this morning. The new delivery date is three weeks from today."

Jerry stops talking. No one else speaks. The room is dead. Just a little air blowing, a coffee pot gurgling on the credenza, a deep breath.

Tom Winston breaks the silence. "We knew it last week, but we were optimistic that we could overcome some of the problems. It wasn't our fault. Suppliers were late, defective components, a few misunderstandings. We're sure we can have it out within the next three weeks. And, we've learned a lot."

"Some of it was a design change at the last minute," Sidney adds. "We saw a way to improve the product's performance by 20 percent. We made the changes. It will be a much better piece of equipment."

Arthur interjects in an upbeat way. "Look at it this way, Jerry. The customer will get greater performance and more reliability because we have some extra time to make it perfect."

"That's not the point, Arthur," Jerry replies, his voice

strained. "The customer was willing to accept the original performance specs and was expecting the unit installed in their new production line, which is scheduled to start up in five days. The 4900 is the main quality control element in their line. You are telling me that they will suffer a delay of three weeks in their start-up."

Arthur jumps in. "Jerry, you know as well as I do that their start-up date will probably slip because their other suppliers will have had trouble meeting their delivery dates, too. We'll just be one of the crowd, Jerry." He adds, "They won't even notice. Don't you think you're overreacting?"

Jerry reaches in the file lying in front of him on the big rosewood conference table. He removes five sheets of paper and hands one to each of us, keeping one for himself that he reads from:

> *Dear Jerry:*
>
> *We are counting on your organization to deliver your new RF4900 test unit on time. We assume that it went out on Friday, even though our trucker cannot trace the shipment.*
>
> *Please have your technician at our plant in Atlanta on Thursday to complete the installation so we can start up our new production line on Friday. All other equipment is in place.*
>
> *Sincerely,*
> *Violet Worstheimer*

"It couldn't be helped," Sidney says. "You know we want to ship only the best. We saw that we could do better. We had to incorporate the new technology."

"Max, I think I need some help here. I don't know

where to go with this," Jerry says, as he buries his shaking head in his hands.

I walk to the white board on the wall.

"I am going to share a system I use to help people in this kind of situation. I call it a Gap Analysis, but first I want to explain what a gap is."

I draw an inverted triangle. "Can everyone see this?"

They all nod or say yes.

"People take action because they want something. If they perceive that they don't have what they want, then there is something missing. There is a gap between what they want and what they perceive they have.

"To get what they want, they choose a behavior and act to close that gap and make their perceptions look like what they want. Does that make sense so far?" I fill in the Triangle of Choice as I go along.

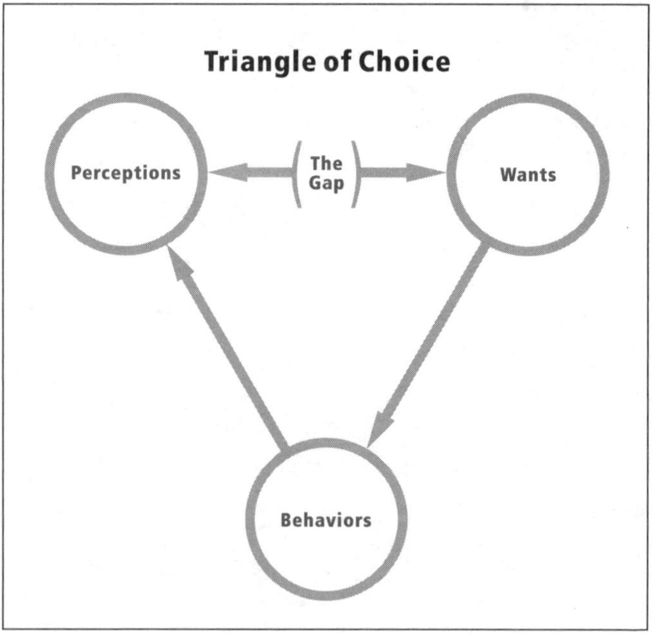

There is no response while people examine the drawing.

"It's really just a closed loop system; is that what you're saying, Max?" Sidney asks. "This looks like control theory. We use it all the time in engineering."

"Yes, exactly, Sidney. It originated with control theory. But we've found that people operate from this triangle or loop, too, just like machines. Do you get this, Arthur? Tom?"

"Yes, so far," Arthur says.

"Keep going," says Tom.

"If we want to change the current situation, we need to work in the present. I want to stick with what our situation is now, how we perceive it in this moment. We can't change the past, although we can learn from it. We can only choose our direction for the future if we work in the present. So let's stick to the current situation. Is that OK with everyone?"

I look at each person. They all nod their agreement.

"We're going to focus on how we perceive the current situation, what we want, and the choices we have at this time. Do you see how those factors relate to the three points in the Triangle of Choice?

"As I understand it, the purpose of this meeting is to find a way to satisfy the needs of your customer. Is that true?"

Everyone says yes.

I go on. "Right now, we don't want to deal with what happened before today unless it will contribute to satisfying your customer today. We are not trying to fix your manufacturing process or the people that run it, at this time.

"We will start with a review of what you just revealed — your current perceptions." I write these on the board as I repeat them. "Please add to the list or suggest corrections as I go along."

1. *The customer expected shipment last Friday.*
2. *We did not ship.*
3. *The product will be delayed three weeks.*
4. *The customer plans to start production in five days.*
5. *The RF4900 is the main quality control component in their production line.*
6. *The RF4900 is the only component missing from the line.*

"Anybody have additions or changes?"

Sidney responds, "There is nothing in there about our desire to give them a better product."

"Will that solve the customer's current problem? No quality control component in their production line?"

"No, I guess not."

"Let's go on with what we all want, here in this moment. Is that OK with everyone?"

No answer, so I move ahead. "What do you want, Jerry?"

"I want to ship the unit as we promised so that it will arrive by Thursday, even if we have to pick up the air freight charges, even if we have to work the next two days and nights continually without sleep so that the 4900 gets shipped. I want to satisfy the customer."

"How about you, Sidney? What do you want now?"

"Look, we do the best we can. We may have some delays up front, but in the long run, we'll be delivering a better instrument."

"Sidney, you referred to the delays you already have and what the company will have in the future. Let's deal with the immediate situation. What do you want, now, taking into consideration what Jerry wants and what the customer needs?"

"If I had known how critical this delivery was, I would not have changed the spec on that circuit board two weeks ago. I thought this was like all the other delivery requests customers make. We often fail to deliver on time and usually it's no problem."

I see the anguish in Jerry's face as he responds silently to each comment.

"Sidney, you have not answered my question. There is nothing we can do about the past. What do you want in this moment that might help Jerry and the customer?"

"I'd like to deliver the product sooner, but I can't see how."

Tom made an offer. "If it would matter at all, I am willing to get people to work around the clock to make it happen. I would like to do that now, but we changed that one part to get the added performance and it will not be here for two weeks. My prototype team can assemble most of the modules in the system in twenty-four hours. We can have it ready and waiting for that new circuit board when it arrives."

"Tom, that's a great solution, but we are focusing on what you want, not on solutions. I do not want to shortcut this process. If we do what you suggest, what would we accomplish? What is it you want to get out of this effort?"

"Oh, I want to give the customer high-quality service and support," Tom replies.

"Good. That's what you want and we will consider solutions a little later.

"Arthur, what do you want?"

"I'd like Jerry to call the customer, and just explain the situation. Tell them how much better off they will be when the faster unit comes in. Eventually, they'll make up the lost time. Why don't you do that, Jerry?"

"We could ask Jerry to do that, Arthur. And we can collect more information about what we all want before we put Jerry on the phone with the news, bad or otherwise. We may generate many alternatives in this process that could work more effectively to get us all what we want."

Arthur responds, "I'd like to go back to two weeks ago, when engineering came up with this new approach. It was simple, but we should have talked to Jerry and the customer before we made the change."

"Arthur, we can't go back two weeks. We need to focus on what we can do now."

"I'd like to finish the damn thing and ship it ASAP!" The expression snaps from Arthur's lips as one word, rather than as letters. "That's what I want. ASAP, just like Jerry."

"Then you all agree that you want to meet the deadline, even if it takes a huge effort?"

All heads nod.

I paraphrase and summarize where we are. "We agree that we are late shipping the equipment. We all want to do whatever it takes to deliver the 4900 by Thursday or as soon as possible. Does anybody have anything to add?"

No one speaks. I ask each person in the room for their agreement, just to confirm their position.

Jerry says, "Yes, of course."

Tom and Sidney also agree.

Arthur says, "Look, I have previous commitments. I don't have much time so I may have to leave. Jerry, Tom, and Sidney are very capable of working this out. I believe in empowering my people."

"Does that mean you agree, Arthur?"

"Yes, of course. I thought I made it clear that I support these guys."

12

Closing the Gap

Poise in the face of paradox is a key not only to effectiveness, but to sanity in a rapidly changing world.

—Michael J. Gelb

"Let's make a list under each of these headings to see where we stand." I write two headings on the board.

After a few minutes with everyone contributing, we narrow down the list to look like this:

GAP ANALYSIS	
Present Situation (Perceptions)	**What We Want (Wants)**
Missing new circuit board	*Deliver on time*
Receive board next week	*Do whatever it takes*
Customer will be unhappy	*Jerry convince customer to accept late delivery*
Can't ship until board received	*Control costs*
Did not deliver on time	*Make best choice together*
Customer expected shipment on Friday	*Provide excellent customer service*

We go over each item in these two lists to determine which we can control and which are beyond our control and influence.

"Can we control the fact that we do not have the new circuit board?" I ask.

"It's too late now. We don't have it. Maybe we can get the supplier to move more quickly," Sidney suggests.

"What you are saying is that the missing board is just a fact of life, a predicament, which is beyond our control."

"We don't have it, so we have to wait for it," Tom adds.

"Can we control the delivery of the new circuit board?" I ask.

"We've already called the supplier. He says he's waiting for a component that is being built this week that goes on the circuit board. He assures me that it will be shipped to them from Asia on Friday by air," Sidney says.

"What else can we do?" Jerry asks. "Have we explored other alternatives?"

"Not really," Sidney replies. "I don't think there are any. We need that board and the supplier can't finish it until they get the part they need."

"Have you talked to the supplier to see if they are willing to get our board out immediately once they get the part from Asia?" Jerry asks.

"No, I did not talk to them about that. It would probably be a good idea," Sidney replies.

I summarize. "What you are saying, Sidney, is that there is nothing we can control to get that part from Asia sooner. But we can possibly influence the supplier to get the circuit board out faster once they have received the part. Is that true?"

"Yes, I'm sure they will do it for us."

Jerry asks, "Will you do that? Will you call the supplier?"

"Oh, yes. I will right now. Let me use the phone and see what he can do."

"Sidney, let's go through this process first. See if we come up with something else, OK?" I ask.

He nods his agreement.

I go on. "It looks like we may be able to do something about the delivery of the new circuit board. Get it faster. That is somewhat of a change in our original perception of getting the part late next week. We may be able to get it sooner.

"What about the customer's unhappiness; can we do something about that?"

"I think the customer will be unhappy with anything we say except that we are going to have the 4900 online this week." Jerry points at the calendar on the wall as he talks. "The only thing we can do to avoid their anger will be to deliver on time. I may be able to lessen the impact by sharing what we are doing to get this handled, but I am going to get reamed over our failure."

"What you are saying is that you can have some influence on the degree of the customer's unhappiness."

"Maybe. But I am not going to call them until we know where we stand later today. If I make a promise, I want to keep it."

"Let's go on. The next item under Present Situation is Can't ship until board received. Is there anything we can do about that? Can we change or influence this situation?"

Tom says, "Doesn't make any sense to ship an incomplete, untested unit."

Jerry asks, "Can we make the conveyor belt on our unit operate without the missing circuit board? If that is possible, we can install the 4900 so that they can run their production line. It may not do the testing they bought it for, but it will serve as a conveyor. Fill the gap in their production line."

"Yes, we can do that," Tom says. "It will cost us a lot and we will have to send a technician to their plant to make the final installation and test when the circuit board comes in. It will take a bit longer and they will probably want us to do it at night so we don't interrupt their production."

Arthur had been quiet for a while. "I need to control the costs around here. We've been tightening our belts a lot in the last few months and this will send a bad message to the troops. I don't know if I want to do it."

Jerry rises from his seat, but I hold up my hand to stop him. "Arthur, you indicated you wanted to get this done ASAP, to use your expression. Is that true?"

"Yes, I guess you're right there. But I did not say I wanted to run my cost controls into the ground doing it."

Jerry replies, his voice rising two octaves, the words flying out like machine gun fire. "This customer will spend as much as $500,000 with us in the next twelve months. If we don't work to satisfy them, then my sales forecast will be short that amount or more, Arthur. Then what will you do with your costs? And what about the customer's costs? I think sales volume and customer retention need to be part of your considerations."

"Don't exaggerate, Jerry," Arthur fires back. "We won't lose the customer. Anyway, I'll go along with the added expense. Just keep it under control, Tom."

I step in again. "Arthur, what exactly are you wanting Tom and Jerry to agree to?"

"I just want them to agree to minimize the costs. I don't want people going off willy-nilly, spending without thinking of the consequences to the company. Let's give the customer what they need without spending more than what is absolutely necessary."

"Does everybody agree to minimize the expenses?"

I get three affirmative answers from Jerry, Tom, and Sidney.

Jerry asks, "Does everyone agree that satisfying the customer is our first priority?"

Tom and Sidney acknowledge their agreement. Arthur grunts.

I ask, "Does that mean yes, Arthur?"

"Yes. OK. Yes, get on with it."

"Let's look at what we can do about our wants. We wanted to deliver on time. Has that changed in any way?"

Sidney answers, "If we can get them to accept the unit as it is now, we partially meet that criteria."

"Anybody else have a point of view about that?"

No one answers.

"What about doing whatever it takes?"

Jerry says, "It sounds like we have an agreement on that. And on the next one, I'll call the customer as soon as Sidney gets a commitment from our supplier. I think the customer will still be unhappy, but cooperative."

"We've agreed on keeping costs to a minimum. Do you think this has been a good example of working together to create a solution we can all live with?"

Tom says, "Yes, we just have to keep it up."

Sidney adds, "I think you've been a great help, Max. I like this Gap Analysis. You can see all the forces at work, what we perceive, and what we want. Oh, and I want to satisfy the customer and keep working with everyone to get the product delivered."

Arthur and Jerry agree.

"Let's add another 'want' at the end here. We want to deliver the system without the new part. That eliminates the gap between what we perceive we have and what we want. Any questions?"

Jerry makes a suggestion. "I would like to review what we're agreeing to do here. I want to have explicit agreements. Is that OK?"

In the next few minutes, we review all the details, creating firm agreements with follow-up times and dates for each.

We write them on a white board and then on paper so that Arthur, Tom, Sidney, Jerry, and I all have copies.

Sidney agrees to call the supplier immediately to expedite the assembly and shipment of the missing circuit board. He agrees to notify Jerry of the result within an hour.

Tom agrees to get his people working on the final assembly and the packing of the 4900 so that it will be ready for shipment within the next twenty-four hours. He says he will be back to Jerry within one hour, too.

Jerry agrees that he will call the customer as soon as Sidney and Tom report the results of their conversations with the supplier and company technicians.

Arthur agrees to the overtime, air freight, and travel expenses for the technicians.

Jerry agrees to report the results of his conversation with the customer.

Within one hour Tom and Sidney are back to Jerry with news no one ever expected. It seems that the supplier had completed assembling a circuit board based on the original specifications and that board was sitting on the supplier's shelf ready to ship.

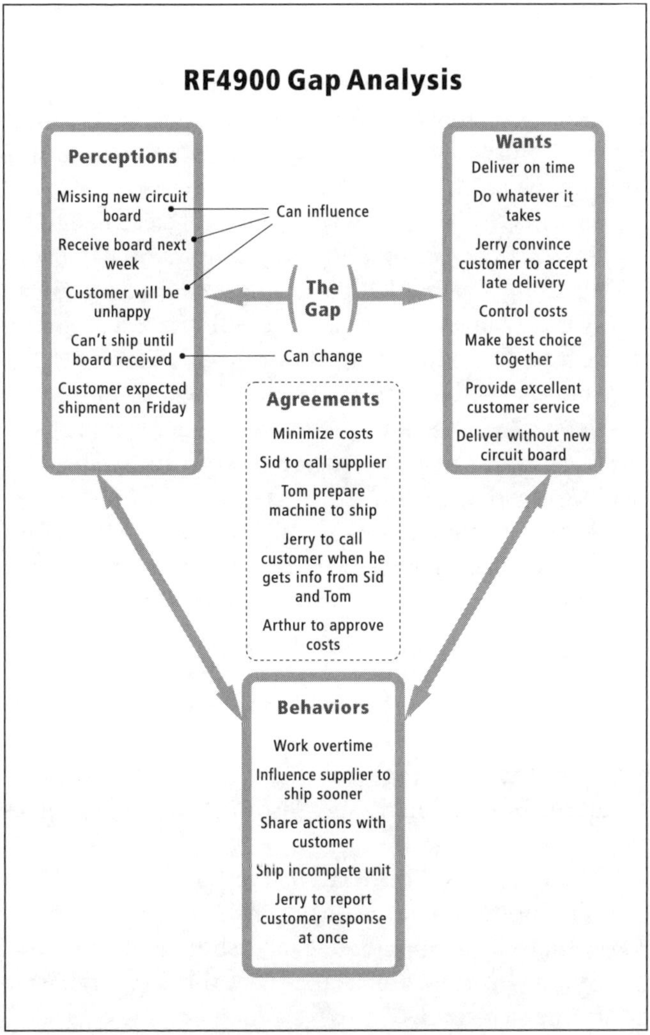

It will still be necessary to assemble the 4900 with a round-the-clock effort, and the unit will be shipped by air with technicians working on-site to install and test it. The customer will get the machine on time and in working order.

At the end of the day I meet with Jerry.

"Max, I liked that process. The Gap Analysis used everything you showed me about the Triangle of Choice, the Procedures That Lead to Change, Locus of Control, and the Microdot of Control. And the use of explicit agreements really clarified what our next steps had to be.

"It was a great demonstration of how you can lead a group using this model. If we all get trained in how to apply the Triangle of Choice, we will create a common context to deal with many of our biggest problems. I'm looking forward to our continuing conversations."

"Jerry, if you stick to the model, keep bringing people back to it, you will be using a very effective tool for leading any discussion."

"It may be a good idea if we had some formal training for all the managers in the business unit." Jerry asks, "Could you influence Arthur to authorize that, Max?"

"I have an appointment with him tomorrow. Is there something you can do to influence Arthur yourself?"

"I see the value that training can bring to the organization. But Arthur is such a bean counter. He does not value training."

"What do you think Arthur does value?"

"The bottom line. Money. Profit and cash flow. I know that for sure because he talks about it all the time."

"What you are saying is that he wants to create more profits and cash flow."

"Yes, that's right."

"Have you asked him about training in the past?"

"I have. He approves of sales training. He sees the value in it. He has rejected everyone else's requests for training. People have tried for leadership training, effective meetings, communication. Thumbs down on all of them," Jerry says.

"What have you tried to get him to buy-in on other training?"

"Nothing. I only ask about sales training?"

"What could you do, Jerry?"

"I could prepare a plan, maybe with your help, and make a proposal. Knowing he equates everything to the bottom line, I need to show him how the training will generate more profit or increase our cash flow. Do you have any figures you can share with me, Max? Anything that shows an impact on the bottom line?"

"As a matter of fact, I do, Jerry. I have letters from directors and other high-level executives in other divisions. I have my own data and I also have data that was generated by our CFO. All of it is positive. I will be happy to share it with you."

"I'd like that." He smiles. "When will you send it to me? I need a specific agreement." We laugh.

"I will have my assistant send it to you tomorrow, Jerry."

"Max, don't make a big deal out of the training tomorrow in your meeting with Arthur. Just mention it as a possibility. Kind of lay the groundwork. I will put together a proposal with your help and make a formal pitch sometime in the next month. Is that OK with you, Max?"

"Sounds like a good start to me, Jerry."

"Is there anything else you want to discuss today about the process?"

13

A Way of Being?

Self-creation either spirals inward to become smaller and more certain, or reaches out into the world to discover newness.

—Margaret J. Wheatley and Myron Kellner-Rogers

"Yes," Jerry says, "there is one thing. I noticed that you stayed pretty even and centered during most of the discussion. I was really agitated at one point. If you had not interrupted me, I would have said something that could have disrupted the process. What can I do to achieve your kind of easygoing approach, Max?"

"The question you need to be asking yourself is one I ask all the time: Who do I want to be in this situation? I ask myself this question in almost every encounter with other people. It is a habit that took a while to develop and use."

"Who do I want to be? You mentioned the same thing this morning. Sounds like you expect people to change their basic nature to accommodate every situation.

I think that would take a lot of practice."

"Jerry, I want you to access your basic nature, to call forth your ideal picture of yourself.

"It does take practice and you are probably doing it unconsciously anyway. Do you vary your approach with different people, depending on the situation, Jerry?"

"Sure. I try to adapt my style to theirs, especially when I am in front of a customer in a selling situation. If you don't adapt, you end up losing a lot of sales."

"There's no difference in a nonselling situation, or whenever you want to influence or lead others. You are selling the other person or people on your point of view, so you want to adapt your approach to what will work best. When you speak, you lead. People follow what you say. You follow what they say. We are always leading and following.

"Some situations call for strength and directness; some for a gentle hand. Other situations call for a high degree of responsibility and seriousness. Some are best handled with a lighthearted approach. You are the judge, and you make the choice.

"You said you wanted to be even and centered. Let's do one more exercise that can help you get a handle on this concept.

"Remember this morning when you described your frustration with Arthur and we designed a new behavior?"

"Yes, something about Total Behavior, wasn't that it?"

"Yes, and do you remember that all behaviors are made up of four elements?"

"Yes, it was doing, thinking, feeling, and physiology."

"Perfect, Jerry. We can use this information to look at your current behaviors and then design a new behavior you can learn to use when you think it will be more effective. We do a Total Behavior Analysis.

"Let's look at what is going on for you when you are not acting in an even, centered, and easygoing manner.

"What were you doing in that moment I interrupted you in the meeting, Jerry?"

"Let me think about this. See if I can recreate the image." He looks up toward the ceiling, searching his memory.

"My hands were balled up in fists. I was feeling like a guitar string ready to snap. And . . ."

"Your hands were balled in a fist, you were feeling angry, and your body was tense. What were you doing?"

"I was talking loudly. Almost yelling. My volume was increasing with each exchange. I was pointing my finger at times. My voice was strained and I was talking fast."

I wrote these on the white board as he spoke so he could see them. "Any other things you were doing?"

"Not that I can think of."

"What kind of language were you using? Was it direct or accusatory? Friendly or businesslike?"

"Oh, I would say businesslike. I even used some of the Triangle of Choice language."

"What were you thinking when all of this was going on?"

"I was thinking that Arthur is a real bean counter with only one thing on his mind, controlling costs; that Sid has more excuses than my teenage son; that Tom is very cooperative. I guess I was making lots of judgments about them. Not very helpful in figuring out how to influence them.

"I was also thinking that Arthur and Sid do not understand how hard it is to get a customer like Milov.

What it takes to retain them. Customers, I mean.

"I'm a little shocked by my own thoughts. This is frightening. I don't want to be thinking this way."

"Anything else you were thinking, Jerry?"

"I wanted to quit. Leave them in the lurch and let them deal with it."

"How were you feeling?"

"Angry. As I said before, uptight, vengeful, disgusted, unappreciated, overwhelmed. Generally pissed off. Frustrated."

"Any other feelings, Jerry?"

"I am not only reporting this. I am feeling the whole thing all over again. I'm getting agitated and pissed."

"I'm glad you see that, because it is one of the most valuable parts of this exercise — recreating the behavior in a controlled environment so that you can really experience the cost to you and others. Do you get that, Jerry?"

"Big time. I mean, I am getting the same feelings I had in the real event. Just thinking and talking about it."

"What was going on in your body?"

"It's going on now. I was hot, sweating. My heart was thumping harder than normal. I could hear it at times. I had a bit of a headache and my neck was tight.

"This process, what did you call it, Max? Total Behavior?"

"Yes."

"It makes the whole thing real all over again."

"What do you perceive about it, Jerry?"

"This is not who I want to be, Max. I am doing myself more harm than good and I am not getting what I really want. I want people to listen to me when I'm frustrated. Take action and get things done. I think I can get more of what I want if I am more easygoing."

"What do you mean by easygoing, Jerry?"

"If I don't act out my anger so overtly. It probably scares some people. Has the opposite effect to what I want. I need to be more of a salesperson in these situations. Not be so demanding."

"Not necessarily, Jerry. Sometimes you need to be firm and demanding. And you can do that with a lot less stress on yourself. Can you see that?"

"Maybe. I'm not sure. What do I have to do?"

"We're not talking about doing here, Jerry. We are describing a way of being that will drive what you do.

"Let's design a new behavior, one that you can substitute for the old one.

"I want to caution you, though. The change will not happen overnight. You have to work at it. Judging from what you have told me, you will get many opportunities to practice."

Jerry nods his head in agreement. "I understand, Max. This seems like a long-term project."

"When I train groups of people to use this work, it takes four or five four-hour sessions to get up a head of steam. Then people seem to catch on and start using it. It becomes part of their daily living, especially when others are using it around them. When we get the other managers, supervisors, and the staff people using the model, it will become easier and effective very fast.

"Now we know the behavior you were choosing. Let's give it a name. What would you call it, Jerry?"

"That's an easy one, Max. Anger. I am angry when I choose that behavior."

"Excellent, Jerry. Who do you want to be?"

"I want to be easygoing. To be someone who listens well: really hears and sees what people want and choose. I want to be the kind of person who shows genuine concern for others. I want to lead people, whether they work for me or not, to connect their behaviors and choices to the needs and goals of the organization so we can create results together. Ultimately, that is what we are here for. I want to be firm and gentle at the same time."

"Why do you want to be that way? What will motivate you to change?"

"That's pretty easy, too. I want people to work with me, to have a desire to support the organization without my having to pound on them, to join me willingly without defensiveness or their own anger. Do With is what you called it. That's what I want to produce: Do With."

"Who would you have to be to produce Do With?"

Jerry goes right to it without any hesitation. "I would be asking a lot of questions. I would keep people on track. Listen more and talk less. Loosen up. Talk slower. Unclasp my hands and maybe be less agitated. Not point at anyone.

"I would be thinking that these people want to do the right thing. They just have a different context. A different point of view, like Arthur wanting to control costs. I have to recognize what they want and tie it to what I want. I need to lead them with my words and actions. That's what I want to be thinking."

"How do you want to feel, Jerry?"

"I remember you telling me that I cannot directly control my feelings and physiology. They change as a result of the changes I make in my thinking and doing. If I were thinking and doing what I described in this new behavior, then I would be feeling more centered, less agitated, more peaceful, and maybe even friendly. I may even feel happy and satisfied." He smiles at the thought.

"I might take it all as a typical sales challenge rather than thinking that Arthur and Sid were my adversaries. I'd add that to my thinking, Max."

"What about your physiology?"

"Oh, loose, no pounding heart. Not if I was thinking and doing what I said I would do. I would be calm."

"Anything else, Jerry?"

"Max, this is enough. I can see already that this is a matter of choice. Before I go into any inflammatory situation — excuse me — into *any* situation, I need to be asking myself who I want to be. Take some time to figure out what I want to be doing and thinking. What I want to feel, both emotionally and physically.

"And I don't have to label the situation either. I have a choice as to how I perceive each situation, even when it may be potentially stressful."

"That's great, Jerry. When I first started using Lead Management, I was having a dispute with another manager. I was preparing a nasty, threatening letter and getting angrier as I wrote. I observed how agitated I was as I wrote, and I suddenly realized how it was affecting me, how uptight I was, full of emotion.

"I put the letter aside, wanting to find another way to deal with the situation. I was reading a book about meditation, and I got to a part about compassion.

"I realized I wanted to be compassionate with this guy. His name was Bob. He was always arguing over every detail and refused to help anyone else unless he wanted something. I wouldn't trade one minute of my life for his. I felt this great sadness for him. A life full of anger and distrust. What a way to live.

"I needed to influence Bob so that I could get my job done. I designed a behavior to deal with him. I did a Total Behavior Analysis for myself and then I gave it a name. I called it compassion and I revisited that analysis frequently. I practiced it with Bob every time I saw him. Whenever I ran into Bob, I would repeat the word 'compassion' several times to myself to trigger who I wanted to be.

"I made the choice to start using this new behavior with other people who were angry like Bob. The behavior did not always get me what I wanted. But it took away much of the pain and frustration of working with angry people.

"I worked on the behavior persistently. It took me about six weeks before I could fully integrate the new behavior into my life.

"I want you to give this new behavior of yours a name, Jerry. If you name it, when you study the behavior and analyze how you are using it, you can attach all of what you learn and experience to the name. Make it a simple phrase or a single word. What will you call it?"

"I'll call it quiet influence. I want to be quiet inside as much as possible, and my actions are always about influencing others in these situations. What else can I do to be who I want to be?"

"I have a simple process that worked for me with Bob. Every time I knew I was going into a situation with him, I would sit down at my computer and take a few minutes to go through the Procedures That Lead to Change. I would ask myself what I wanted to accomplish with Bob, the exact outcome. I would look at my perceptions of the situation, the gap, and the alternative behaviors available to me.

"Then I would write out who I wanted to be in the situation. I would describe the doing, thinking, feeling, and physiology. All of this just quick notes. Nothing elaborate.

"Most importantly, after every meeting with Bob, I would take the time to write down what I did well, what I did not do well, how I could be in the future, and what I would do in the future to be who I wanted to be. I would do the Procedures That Lead to Change again, only this time in the past tense. What did I want, what did I do to get it, did it work, and so on.

"It was a process that I extended to my interactions with other people. Soon I could call on a whole list of behaviors that represented who I wanted to be in different situations.

"I identified each with just a word or a phrase, and after many years, most of the time I can be who I intend to be. As much as I would like to say that I have this down cold, I still occasionally choose my angry behavior. I must admit my old habits sometimes get in the way, at least temporarily.

"But, when I apply the system, I am less ineffective and continually learn from my choices, good and bad. That is one of the primary goals in Lead Management: to lead yourself and others toward continuous improvement. The process never ends.

"I've learned to have compassion with myself, to see I am not perfect. Then I can return to the places where I have made mistakes and correct them by being who I want to be — do the self-evaluation and get closer to who I want to be each time. It's part of the practice of Lead Management."

"It sounds like a lot of work, Max."

"It is, Jerry. You cannot change yourself overnight. But you can make huge progress in six weeks or less, and in a year it is possible to change a lot of behaviors. I've seen people do it.

"Will you use this process, Jerry?"

The room is very quiet. Jerry swivels his chair around to face the window, looking toward the horizon, watching the sun above the line of pollution in the distance. He said nothing. It was a couple of minutes before he turned around.

"Max, I'm really looking forward to working with you for a long time to come. When do we meet next?"

14

A Final Thought

Understanding is the booby prize.

—Werner Erhard

Many leaders read a book like this or get a brief exposure to our work through an article or introductory lecture and say they *understand* these principles.

Lead Management is a practice. You cannot be a lead manager by reading this book or listening to a lecture. You can only reap the benefits of these principles by actively using them and experimenting with them.

Sometimes you will be successful. Sometimes you will fail. If you self-evaluate using the principles of Lead Management, you will improve your skills and become a lead manager.

Understanding is never enough. Lead Management will always be a practice you work at every day.

Triangle of Choice
The Procedures That Lead to Change and Other Key Concepts

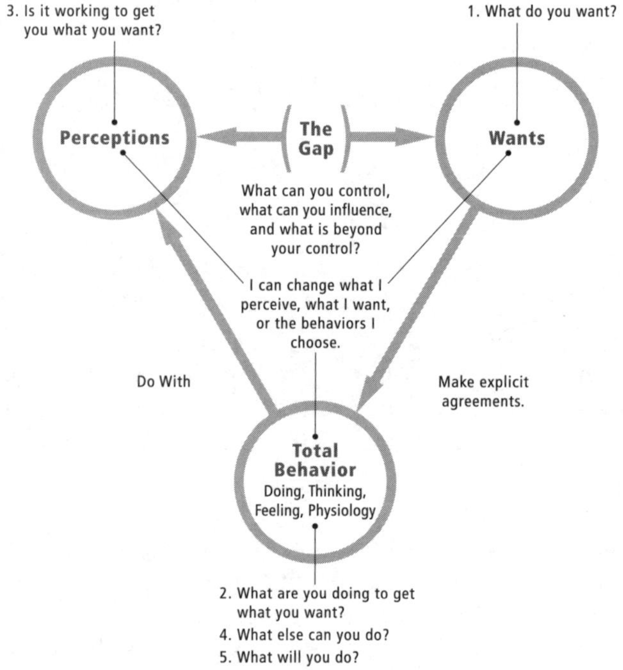

APPENDIX

LEAD MANAGEMENT REVIEW

The effectiveness of a leader is related to the continual improvement of the leader's mental models.

—HANOVER INSURANCE CREDO

- Lead managers make deliberate choices after carefully self-evaluating. They lead other people to do the same. They listen and observe, using a model of human behavior that guides their thoughts and actions.

- Our Lead Management model is based on the Triangle of Choice.

- We receive information from our senses, and combine that information with what we already know to form our perceptions. Most perceptions are based more on what we already know than on what we think we see, hear, touch, taste, and smell.

- We can deliberately choose or change what we perceive.

- In every moment, we are comparing what we perceive with what we want. If there is a difference between what we want and what we perceive we have, then there is a gap.

- We can deliberately choose or change what we want.

- If the gap gets our attention, if it is important to us, then we choose a behavior to close the gap.

- Every behavior we choose is an attempt to close a gap.

- We call behaviors Total Behaviors. Every behavior has four components: doing, thinking, feeling, and physiology.

- We can directly change, or choose what we do and what we think. We cannot directly change our feelings and our physiology, but we can influence them indirectly by changing what we do and what we think.

- A feeling is a signal. We get to choose our reaction to that signal. Our reaction does not have to be automatic, although it may feel that way. Our reaction is a choice.

- We can deliberately choose or change our behavior.

- The behaviors we choose do not always get us what we want. We sometimes choose ineffective behaviors.

- Perceptions, wants, and behaviors make up the three corners of the Triangle of Choice.

- We can deliberately choose or change all three of these components: our perceptions, wants, and behaviors.

- In any situation, we can ask ourselves what we want, what we perceive, and what behaviors we are choosing to get what we want.

- In any situation, we can ask other people what they want, what they perceive, and what behaviors they are choosing to get what they want.

- When we ask ourselves what we want, what we perceive, or what behaviors we are choosing to get what we want, then we are self-evaluating.

- When we ask other people what they want, what they perceive, and what behaviors they are choosing to get what they want, we are helping them self-evaluate.

- Self-evaluation is an effective tool we can use to lead people to results and improve our own.

- The five questions included in the Procedures That Lead to Change are designed to help us self-evaluate using the Triangle of Choice as our map. They are:

    1. *What do I want? (Wants)*
    2. *What am I doing to get what I want? (Behaviors)*
    3. *Is it working to get me what I want? (Perception)*
    4. *What else can I do? (Behaviors)*
    5. *What will I do? (Behaviors)*

- You can lead other people through the questions by changing the pronoun:

    1. *What do you want?*
    2. *What are you doing to get it?*
    3. *Is it working?*
    4. *What else can you do?*
    5. *What will you do?*

- When we use the Procedures That Lead to Change, we want to spend a lot of time asking and answering the first four questions before we go on to the fifth. After we have generated alternatives and evaluated which will create what we want, we make a plan. The plan is generated by the fifth question: What will you do?

- We can ask these questions in many different ways. We can restate the question What do you want? in over a hundred different ways. Here are just four examples:

    1. *What is your ultimate goal in this situation?*
    2. *What are you trying to achieve?*
    3. *What were you hoping to create when you did that?*
    4. *What result did you aim for?*

- We can only control ourselves and, to some extent, what we create. We can influence other people and situations. Most of what happens in the world is out of our control and beyond our ability to influence.

- When we blame other people and events for the results we've created through our own choices of behavior, then we are operating from an external Locus of Control.

- When we are accountable for our part in creating results, we are operating from an internal Locus of Control.

- When we operate from an internal Locus of Control, we take responsibility for our behaviors and perceptions.

- People attribute the ownership of a meeting to the person who is leading the meeting.

- Meetings belong to the participants, as well as to the leader. All participants are cooperatively responsible for the results a meeting produces.

- Responsibility is learning to choose effective behaviors to get what you want and be the person you want to be while you assist others to learn to choose effective behaviors to get what they want.

- We create Do For when we do things for people that they should be doing for themselves. In the process, we rob them of the opportunity to learn what they need to learn to be effective in their jobs. This leads them to feel entitled and we become overburdened with work other people need to be doing for themselves. We also lose credibility.

- After we Do For over time, we begin to resent the burden and then we do something to the other person that comes out of our own frustration and resentment. We ignore them, put them down, give them a poor review, and blame them for failing to do what we want them to do, even though we never received their agreement to do it in the first place. This is Do To behavior.

- We choose a loop of Doing For, Doing To, and then back to Do For.

- The alternative to the Do For/Do To loop is Do With.

- Do With is taking responsibility for what we want, respecting others and what they want, and supporting them to take responsibility for what they want, all of it connected to the goals of the organization and the team.

- If we are guilty of Do For, we need to apply the Procedures That Lead to Change to our own behaviors first. We need to figure out what we want when we are Doing For and answer the remaining four questions so we can support the other person to do what they have to do.

- Support may take the form of guiding the other person in a self-evaluation process where they look at what they want and what they perceive they have. Where is their gap?

- We want them to look at the behaviors they are choosing to get what they want in relation to the tasks and responsibilities of their jobs.

- We use the Procedures That Lead to Change to help them evaluate their choices.

- In the process, we may choose to share our own self-evaluation with those we want to help.

- Do With includes making clear and explicit agreements. You cannot hold people accountable for a result they have never agreed to produce.

- Effective agreements include an early warning system — progress reports that give us fair notice of a problem.

- Making, keeping, and renegotiating agreements are key elements of creating accountability.

- Accountability is getting people to connect their choices of wants, perceptions, and behaviors with the results they produce. It is taking ownership for the consequences of those choices in keeping or failing to keep our agreements with ourselves and with other people.

- In this context, ownership means we do not blame, deny, or defend what we've created as a result of our choices. We made the choices and we created the results.

- Sometimes events happen beyond our control and influence that prevent us from living up to our agreements. We can still be responsible and accountable by making early notification to those who will be affected and by renegotiating our agreements.

- Gap Analysis is an effective tool for determining what we need to change to create the results we want.

- In a Gap Analysis, we list what we perceive we have in a situation and what we want. The differences between what we perceive and what we want represent our gaps.

- We look at each perception and each want and ask if they are within our control, our influence, or beyond our control or influence.

- We identify the current behaviors we are choosing to close each gap, and we evaluate each to see if it is effective.

- We create alternative behaviors for each gap and evaluate if they will do a better job than what we are already choosing.

- After we generate those alternatives, we choose a course of action.

- Our focus is on the positive present and the future. We only talk about the past if we can learn something that will help us deal with the present and the future. We do not look for excuses.

- We can examine our behaviors by doing a Total Behavior Analysis. In any situation, we can observe or look back on what we were doing, thinking, feeling, and the body sensations we experienced in the moment (physiology).

- We can design a new behavior by asking ourselves what we want to be thinking, doing, and feeling in a specific situation. After we design a new behavior, we can plan to use it in a deliberate manner.

- We can help others design a new behavior by leading them through the same process.

- People are always doing the best they can in any given moment.

- Lead Management replaces boss management. Boss management will never produce the long-term results that are produced by Lead Management.

- Lead Management is a way of being. As leaders, we continually self-evaluate, asking ourselves, Who do I want to be in this situation? We create a detailed picture of who we want to be, what we want, what we perceive, and the behaviors we will choose that will reflect who we want to be.

- We always consider how our choices will support our accountabilities, commitments, and our personal and organizational results.

- We lead other people to do the same.

- Lead Management is a process of learning and guiding others to learn how our choices and daily behaviors impact the bottom line and create a productive work environment.

- We are all leaders and we are all managers. We just lead and manage different things.

- Lead Management is created in conversations between people. When we speak, we lead. Every word we say leads those who listen. How we listen impacts the effectiveness of our speaking. When we listen to others, they are leading us.

- Lead managers are acutely aware of the power of speaking.

- Lead managers model what they expect from other people.

- Lead Management is a way of being that incorporates all these principles and more, through the conscious application of the Triangle of Choice and the other processes described in the conversation between Maxine and Jerry.

ACKNOWLEDGMENTS

We acknowledge the following people for their contributions to the creation of this book. Our partner, Deb Turner, for her insights. Our writing coach, Bruce Gelfand, for his help in finding our voices. Our friends and colleagues for their contributions and peer evaluations: Ellen Blakeley, Ron Ernst, Bill Fox, Howard Kropf, Ted Larkins, Beth Nelson, and the many leaders and workers who shared their lives, thoughts, and actions with us over the years. Every moment with them was a learning experience.

With special thanks we acknowledge our editor, Barbara Coster of Cross-t.i Copyediting/Proofreading for her fine work on the manuscript.

Guy Gabriele and Jeanne Spencer of Idea Engineering provided outstanding creativity and responsiveness in designing the book and the cover.

INDEX

ABOUT THE AUTHORS

Jill Morris is a corporate trainer, executive coach, and consultant who has taught thousands of people to apply the Lead Management Model in practical ways in all kinds of environments, from Fortune 500 companies to small businesses.

Steve Morris is an entrepreneur, consultant, and coach who has worked as an owner, manager, and active investor in more than twenty distinct businesses. He is a behavioral analyst and consultant who helps organizations assess, select, and develop high performers at every level of business.

Jill and Steve are owners of ChoiceWorks, Inc., a corporate training, coaching, and assessment firm providing services to clients throughout the United States and Canada. They have offices in San Diego, California and Tucson, Arizona.

CREATE A LEAD MANAGEMENT CULTURE IN YOUR ORGANIZATION

Whether you work for a large international organization, the local plant of a big company, or a small to medium-sized business, ChoiceWorks, Inc. can help you put the principles of Lead Management to work in practical ways to produce increased productivity and greater satisfaction.

The ChoiceWorks team develops and delivers customized training programs targeted to achieve your organization's specific goals.

We have produced outstanding results in numerous companies in the United States.

To learn more about putting Lead Management to work in your company, look us up at *www.choiceworks.com* or call Steve or Jill Morris at (619) 450-6777.